NARRATIVE AND MORALITY
A Theological Inquiry

NARRATIVE
and
MORALITY

A Theological Inquiry

Paul Nelson

THE PENNSYLVANIA STATE
UNIVERSITY PRESS
UNIVERSITY PARK AND LONDON

Library of Congress Cataloging-in-Publication Data

Nelson, Paul, 1952–
Narrative and morality.

Bibliography: p.
Includes index.
1. Christian ethics—History—20th century.
2. Story-telling (Christian theology)
3. Theology—Methodology. I. Title.
BJ1231.N44   1987   241'.01'8   86-43034
ISBN 0-271-00485-1

To my mother, Helen T. Nelson,

and in memory of my father, Everett W. Nelson, 1909–1967

CONTENTS

ACKNOWLEDGMENTS

Begun as a dissertation presented to the faculty of Yale University in 1984, this book manifests my indebtedness to those with whom I was privileged to study. Margaret Farley, Hans Frei, Jon Gunnemann, David Kelsey, George Lindbeck, Wayne Meeks, and John Reeder contributed in various ways to its writing, revision, and publication. For fifteen years of instruction, guidance, and friendship going back to my undergraduate days at Princeton University, I owe a special debt of gratitude to Gene Outka, who supervised the dissertation and, along with Paul Ramsey, first stimulated my interest in theological ethics. Both of them remain my teachers.

Thanks are also due to Stanley Hauerwas for his detailed and gracious comments on my work; to my colleagues and friends in the Lutheran Church in America's Department for Church in Society who sustained me from 1982 to 1984, especially Gerry Puelle, whose secretarial support surpassed all expectation and any just dessert; to Robert Wilken for his helpful conversation during the year I taught at the University of Notre Dame; to Rosemarie Burley for her skillful retyping of the final manuscript; to Philip Winsor and Kathleen Roos, my editor and copyeditor at Penn State Press; and in the largest measure to my wife Susan for her patient encouragement, editorial judgment, production assistance, and, most of all, companionship.

Springfield, Ohio
September 1986

1

INTRODUCTION

There has been much talk recently among theologians, philosophers, historians, and literary critics about the role of narrative, or story, in shaping self-understanding. The literature generated by these discussions is both rich and diverse. Some writers assert the general thesis that the concept of story, or narrative, is a form of understanding *sui generis* that is fundamental to all historical thought and knowledge. Thus, to understand any historical event or form of thought (including ethical theories), one must comprehend it in the context of the narrative or narratives of which it is a part. Certain moral philosophers regard story as foundational, not only to the understanding of a moral tradition, but to the moral views of individuals. There are moral theologians who concur with this formal claim about morality as a human phenomenon and propose to use narrative to explicate the material distinctiveness of the Christian moral life. For them, it is the Christian story that provides the paradigms, metaphors, and concepts that determine adherents' vision and thus shape Christian character. Some students of scripture make the more limited and particular proposal that narrative be revived as a way of construing the Old and New Testaments for theological purposes.

The uses of narrative appearing in this literature are various. My intention is to sort and explore the different kinds of claims made on behalf of narrative and to identify the key issues raised. My hope is that the result will prove to be a reliable guide to the literature. Exposition and classification, however, are not my sole objectives. I propose to submit some of the uses of narrative to critical analysis. As might be expected, not all of the heterogeneous approaches to narrative are of equal significance or promise. Even the most fruitful are often oversold. Those whose curiosity has been stimulated by the current discussions of narrative and who wish to become conversant may find that this critical while appreciative introduction to the conversation saves them time and helps to focus their efforts most effectively. That, at least, is the author's hope.

My own particular interest, as indicated by the title, is to investigate the usefulness of narrative for the methodology of Christian theological ethics. Nevertheless, at least one-third of the book is devoted to moral philosophy, and that may require a brief explanation. In the first place, interest in narrative among Christian ethicists has been stimulated by recent developments in moral philosophy. While some moral theologians today lament their discipline's dependence upon philosophy, it is hardly a new phenomenon. Second, I do not subscribe to the view that the morphology of Christian ethics is utterly distinctive and fundamentally different from that of non-Christian philosophical or human ethics in general. (Whether the specific *content* of Christian ethics is distinctive is another and controversial matter, as will be seen in a subsequent chapter.) In terms of its shape and method, Christian ethics is a species of the genus 'human ethics'. Thus, it seems appropriate to begin my inquiry by considering the role of narrative in moral philosophy.

Doing so will not, I trust, cause me or the reader to lose his or her bearings toward the ultimate theological objective. Indeed, it will prove advantageous in that, to some extent, the heterogeneous claims regarding narrative and the attendant problems in the philosophical and theological camps are analogous. Issues identified and lessons learned among the moral philosophers will contribute to the investigation of the usefulness of narrative for the methodology of Christian ethics.

Before I provide a prospectus of what is to come, I want to suggest why 'narrative', or 'story', has become an important matter of concern in moral philosophy, theology, and Christian ethics. What accounts for the attention it has been receiving of late? The diversity of appeals to narrative even within a single discipline makes it difficult to generalize, but a few contributing factors are worthy of note.

On the philosophical front, more than a few observers are impressed, frustrated, or embarrassed by the fact that there is so much and such seemingly intractable disagreement on matters of fundamental importance.

According to Alasdair MacIntyre, "we have a number of equally impressive and mutually incompatible recent accounts of the status and justification of moral rules, all of them reviving central themes and doctrines of seventeenth- and eighteenth-century moral philosophy."[1] Little, if any, progress has been made, in his estimation, in resolving these disagreements. Recent moral philosophy has made no substantial contribution either to other areas of philosophical inquiry or to the resolution of a host of practical moral problems in medicine, politics, and economic life. There is simply not enough agreement to allow for the rational adjudication of rival claims.

MacIntyre's is a radical indictment that may or may not be warranted. But it is not idiosyncratic. Many philosophers are dissatisfied with the array of reigning ethical theories. Some are ready to explore new approaches or, as in MacIntyre's own case, to attempt to revive and rehabilitate old conceptions of morality from the distant past. Virtue, character, and the narratives that display and shape them are regarded in some quarters as promising topics for moral philosophy.

Dissatisfaction with the state of moral philosophy is also widespread among Christian ethicists. However, their interest in new ways of conceiving the ethical enterprise is prompted also by discomfort with long-standing tendencies in theological thought. For example, James Gustafson observes that modern Protestant ethics has been dominated by the philosophical assumptions of historicism and existentialism.[2] The former has served to obscure what were once seen as time-, person-, and place-invariant constants in human nature. Even where the faint outline of "immutable" nature is still discernible, the latter philosophical tendency has made it difficult to deduce any moral conclusions from the "givens" of nature. As a result, Protestant ethics has emphasized the moral agent's subjective confirmation of moral directives in the act of existential choice. The moral life has come to be seen as a series of such occasions calling for radical decision. Often, such decisions have been considered in the context of difficult and relatively rare moral quandaries. This emphasis has tended to eclipse concern for the morality of the quotidian. Relatively little attention has been paid to any quality or capacity resident in the moral agent between or beyond these discrete moments of choice. Thus, the traditional emphasis on virtue and character has fallen into neglect. However, as Gustafson notes, a growing number of Protestant ethicists are currently attempting to move beyond this legacy of "subjectivism" and "occasionalism." Attention to the way in which narratives display virtues and shape character is one avenue of this advance.

Theologians (other than those who specialize in theological ethics) have taken up narrative for reasons as diverse as the uses to which they apply it. Those theologians who stand in the tradition of Schleiermacher and nineteenth-century liberalism seek to identify and probe the religious dimension or horizon of human experience in order to demonstrate the perennial relevance of religion and to guide the continuous revision of the religious tradition in appropriate directions. For some, this "turn to the subject" yields the anthropological thesis that narrative is the universal inner form of human experience. Personal identity is said to require an understanding of one's experience as a coherent story. Religious texts or traditions are seen as providing the means by which people can find meaning in their personal stories and orient themselves in relation to the larger world. Current interest in narrativity and religious autobiography serves this liberal theological enterprise.

However, another group of theologians, sometimes denominated as "postliberal," conceive the theological task quite differently. They show little interest in establishing a natural foundation upon which to construct a universally intelligible religious edifice. Their concern is to explicate the meaning Christianity has for its adherents. The meaning is immanent in the tradition, and the theologian's primary work is "intratextual." Eschewing the anthropological thesis and its attendant interest in all sorts of stories and narrative per se, those postliberal theologians who speak of narrative at all do so in a far more restrictive way. For them, narrative represents a way of construing the Bible, as a whole or in part, which is conducive to their display of scripture's normative role in shaping Christian self-understanding and practice.

Of course, theological talk about narrative is not confined to these two schools of academic theology. Conservative "preliberal" theologians, theologically interested biblical scholars, and practitioners of "religion and literature" join in a discussion that shows no signs of abating. The Narrative Interpretation and Christian Theology Group within the American Academy of Religion, formed in 1981, now has a register of more than 120 members from colleges, universities, seminaries, and, in a few cases, churches. The group's annual meetings regularly overflow the assigned rooms. Articles and books concerning narrative continue to proliferate. All of the above is of consequence for this book.

It is probably too early for a conclusive assessment of narrative and religious thought. The debates concerning narrative are still in their early rounds. The issues, as I shall argue, are by no means clear and well defined. Significant participants have yet to produce major constructive statements. Thus, as is inevitably true of attempts to write contemporary history, the status of my contribution to this ongoing discussion must be that of an interim report subject to revision. Nevertheless, it seems to me worthwhile to identify key issues as they stand now, to offer criticisms of some prominent claims in the literature, and to suggest a fruitful direction for future work.

I propose to proceed as follows. In Chapter 2 I shall discuss two theses regarding historical understanding. The first is the claim that to understand one's self it is necessary to discover the story or stories of which one is a part. The second is MacIntyre's proposal that the history of moral philosophy be understood as a narrative. Both the logic of the development of ethical theory and the plausibility of any particular ethical theory depend, according to MacIntyre, upon their being located within a historical narrative. I find his historical narration of the developments by which modern moral philosophy has arrived at its present impasse, in general, to be both illuminating and persuasive.

Chapter 3 examines the relation of narrative to the moral concepts of social groups and individuals. The views of moral philosophers (such as MacIntyre, R. W. Hepburn, Iris Murdoch, R. W. Beardsmore, R. B. Braithwaite, D. Z. Phillips, and H. O. Mounce) who have sought to substitute 'narrative' and 'vision' for traditional accounts of moral rationality will be discussed. Four issues emerge concerning the freedom and autonomy of moral agents, the status of narrative-independent moral rules, and the problem of relativism.

More specifically, if our moral notions are said to arise from the stories that determine who we are, and if the influence of stories is as strong as some claim, then is it possible for agents to criticize, revise, or reject the moralities into which they have been socialized? Do some of the claims regarding narrative's vise-grip on self-understanding compromise autonomy and our freedom to adopt new stories and thus new moral notions? Can we "adopt" stories, or do they adopt and thereby enslave us? Does a narrative model of morality allow for the existence of moral standards or rules that are not dependent upon particular stories? If not, the narrative model of morality would seem to entail relativism. What sort of relativism might this be? I shall argue that attention to narrative, while important, is not so exclusively important as its advocates sometimes claim. There are some universal features of morality (akin to what Bernard Gert calls "the moral rules") that are not narrative-dependent. All of these issues will reemerge in Chapter 7 when I consider the adequacy of a narrative-based theological ethic.

Chapter 4 analyzes MacIntyre's widely influential constructive proposal for the rehabilitation of an ethic of virtue shaped by narrative. Since, without doubt, he is the principal philosophical proponent of narrative ethics, his account merits careful study. Moreover, MacIntyre's views have had a profound influence on the thought of Stanley Hauerwas, the leading exponent of narrative theological ethics, which is the subject of Chapter 7. I shall argue that MacIntyre's claims concerning virtue and narrative do not fit together as comfortably as he supposes. What is problematic in MacIntyre's vision will be shown to be problematic in that of his theological ally.

Before turning to Hauerwas, however, it will be necessary to consider the emergence of narrative in recent theological literature. This is appropriate for two reasons. First, Hauerwas is correct to insist that Christian ethics be understood and conducted as one aspect of the theological enterprise and not as an independent, "neutral" discipline. Furthermore, his interest in narrative, virtue, and character has been stimulated not only by MacIntyre's philosophy but by the discussion of narrative among theologians.

Therefore, in Chapter 5 I shall locate the roots of "narrative theology" in the thought of H. Richard Niebuhr. Divergent uses of narrative will be classified as belonging to either a liberal-universalistic or a postliberal-particularistic tradition. I also wish to engage the current spirited debate between these two traditions concerning the disputed "public" nature of theological discourse and the status of the truth claims afforded by postliberal "intratextual" theology. While my interest is primarily descriptive and analytic, I shall indicate where and why I think the postliberal approach is the more promising. The overall purpose of this chapter is to assess the claim that attention to narrative is fundamental to theological method and to identify its implications for theological ethics.

If the claims of the preceding chapters that narrative is important for our understanding of any morality and that it is especially significant for the work of Christian theology are true, it would seem that narrative ought to offer a way of specifying how scripture is normative in shaping the Christian moral life. In Chapter 6 I shall discuss the notoriously problematic relation between scripture and ethics. After surveying some of the traditional ways scripture has been employed in ethics, I shall consider the suggestion that construing scripture as narrative helps to specify that relation. Narrative will be shown to provide a context for a legitimate (re-)appropriation of some, though by no means all, of the explicitly moral teachings of scripture. Christian ethics, nevertheless, must not be thought identical to either the ethics of the Bible or the ethics of biblical narrative.

Chapter 7 examines Hauerwas's application of the work of Murdoch, MacIntyre, Barth, and Hans Frei in his theological and social ethics. The philosophical issues discussed in Chapters 3 and 4 reemerge along with certain distinctly theological issues: sanctification and the relation between the church and the society of which it is a part. Since Hauerwas is the preeminent champion of narrative in Christian ethics, criticisms of his work are telling.

In a concluding Chapter 8, I shall report the findings of my inquiry and offer my assessment of the usefulness of narrative in theological ethics. Hauerwas's view of marriage and the family will serve as a concrete test case that shows what the narrative approach looks like when it is applied to a specific problem. The limitations of narrative, particularly troublesome in the area of social ethics, are insurmountable. Although it is a necessary focus, attention to narrative does not exhaust the methodological agenda. Narrative, by itself, does not provide an adequate comprehensive account of the Christian moral life. Christian ethics ought not content itself with a coherentism based on narrative. It cannot afford to lose sight of those universal, narrative-independent features of morality identified in Chapter 3. But neither should Christian ethics cling to a non-narrative foundationalism that renders the narrative-dependent features of morality otiose or irrelevant. To argue, as I shall, that Christian ethics stands to profit from both coherentist and foundationalist insights is not an irenic banality. Narrative-dependent and narrative-independent aspects of morality could be combined to form a hybrid account of Christian ethics that would be both viable and hardy. While the working out of this suggestion into a complete description and defense of such an ethics must be the task of another volume—and, perhaps, author—I shall point to some preliminary questions and problems that require further attention.

2

NARRATIVE AND
HISTORICAL UNDERSTANDING

Invocations of narrative, story, fable, and paradigm have recently appeared in the writings of moral philosophers. There they provide alternatives to what have been the dominant themes of twentieth-century Anglo-American moral philosophy. The uses to which the concept of narrative is put by contemporary philosophers are highly diverse. In this chapter and the next two, I shall explore some of the claims advanced under the flag of narrative. The conclusions to be drawn from these philosophical discussions will serve as a foundation for my inquiry into the role of narrative in theological ethics. Uses of narrative in the two disciplines and their liabilities are, to a great extent, analogous. Issues identified here will reappear throughout subsequent chapters.

The fundamental idea underlying the variety of claims made on behalf of narrative is that narrative, or story, is ingredient to understanding the self, social groups, and their histories. According to some philosophers, a moral view is not so much chosen as it is inherited from one's family and from one's religious and political communities; in short, from one's social world. The moralities into which we are socialized are not so much sets of rules or principles as they are collections of stories about human possibilities and paradigms for action. These stories are said to disclose who we are, where we have been, and where we are going, thereby allowing us to locate our position in the larger scheme of things. The narrative context of moral concepts is the subject of the following chapter.

In the present chapter, I shall focus on two theses regarding historical understanding. The first is the claim that to understand one's self it is necessary to discover the story or stories of which one is a part. The second is the thesis that the history of moral philosophy, with its succession of competing theories, can be understood only when it is comprehended within a narrative. Furthermore, it is suggested that to assess the adequacy of any particular moral theory one must consider both the background of its immediate predecessors and the foreground of its social context. The concept of narrative is an umbrella under which some moral philosophers seek a methodology that is less abstract and more historical than that of recent analytic models. I shall begin with the claim about self-understanding.

THE NARRATIVE SELF

There is a tendency in liberalism and positivism to regard the self as being detached from the entanglements of society, history, and even its own past. This liberal self, serene and autonomous, floats freely in the rarefied atmosphere of Reason. Rationality is accorded pride of place at the expense of affectivity and sociality.

A more adequate conception of selfhood is, according to Alasdair MacIntyre, "a concept of a self whose unity resides in the unity of a narrative which links birth to life to death as narrative beginning to middle to end." Similarly, human actions ought not to be seen as isolated bits of behavior independent of the agent's intentions, beliefs, and settings. Rather, they ought to be understood as components of a "narrative history" or an "enacted dramatic narrative in which the characters are also the authors."[1] While acknowledging that we may seem to be assigned certain roles and inserted into a story that pre-exists our appearance, MacIntyre maintains that we are, or at least are capable of being, "co-authors" of our narratives. Despite the fact that we are acted upon and impressed into roles in the dramas of others, we are, nevertheless, able to enact our intentions and thereby to participate in the creation of stories that are uniquely our own. This is a crucial and controverted claim to which I shall return in Chapter 3.

The narrative concept of the self requires that

the narratives which we live out have both an unpredictable and a partially teleological character. If the narrative of our individual

and social lives is to continue intelligibly—and either type of narrative may lapse into unintelligibility—it is always both the case that
there are constraints on how the story can continue *and* that within
those constraints there are indefinitely many ways that it can
continue.[2]

We are accountable to others for the intelligibility of our stories, and they
are accountable to us for that of theirs. According to MacIntyre, the
concepts of narrative, intelligibility, accountability, and personal identity
stand in a relationship of mutual presupposition. None is more fundamental than another, and all are necessary if we are to make sense of ourselves.

HISTORY AS NARRATIVE

The connection between narrative and intelligibility has been recognized
in recent debates among historians and philosophers of history. W. B.
Gallie, for example, contends that "narrative is the form which expresses
what is basic to and characteristic of historical understanding."[3] As historians scrutinize the records of the past, they seek to discern

> a trend or tendency . . . gradually disclosed through a succession of
> events; it is something that belongs to the events which [they] are
> following and no other; it is, so to speak, a pattern quality of those
> particular events. . . . Our appreciation of any historical trend must
> depend upon, or be a resultant of, our following a particular
> narrative, a narrative of events which happened to be arranged in
> such a way that, roughly speaking, they move in some easily described
> relation to some fixed point of reference.[4]

According to Gallie, historical research and writing always contain narratives that "are followable or intelligible in the same general way that all
stories are." For him, "history is a species of the genus Story."[5]

Gallie's view represents a radical rejection of the traditional "covering-
law model" of scientific analysis and explanation.[6] In his estimation,
historians resort to causal explanations of past events only when their
efforts to establish the coherence and "followability" of a narrative fail.
However, as L. O. Mink observes, Gallie's thesis about following an
existent narrative may not help the historian who must *construct* "a narrative backwards from the event to be interpreted by tracing its genesis."[7]

Haskel Fain, another critic of causal explanation, suggests that "the historian may be compared to an editor who must try to preserve an original story while seeking at the same time to increase its intelligibility."[8] According to Fain, the quest for intelligibility requires decision-making procedures regarding the applicability of historical concepts. These criteria for determining what does and does not fit into a given narrative are what opponents of the "history as story" position often find lacking.[9]

The connection Gallie posits between our appreciation of a historical trend and our being able to follow a particular narrative is evident in a recent work of political philosophy. Exploring ideas of liberation and revolution in Western political thought, Michael Walzer observes that throughout history they have been understood as an enactment of the biblical story of the Exodus: "Within the sacred history of the Exodus, [activists and revolutionaries] discovered a vivid and realistic secular history that helped them to understand their own political activity." Through centuries of telling and retelling, the Exodus story "became part of the cultural consciousness of the West—so that a range of political events . . . have been located and understood within the frame it provides." For the historian no less than for the political radical, the Exodus story becomes a powerful metaphor, a story that "makes it possible to tell other stories."[10]

A NARRATIVE OF MORAL THEORY

Further corroboration for Gallie's thesis may be found in MacIntyre's attempt to construct an intelligible story of the history of moral theory in the West. MacIntyre insists that a morality can be understood only when it is examined within the context of a historical narrative:

> Man is in his actions and practice, as well as in his fictions, essentially a story-telling animal. He is not essentially, but becomes through his history, a teller of stories that aspire to truth. But the key question for men is not about their own authorship; I can only answer the question, 'What am I to do?' if I can answer the prior question, 'Of what story or stories do I find myself a part?'[11]

And that is true whether the morality in question be that of an individual, a philosophical school, or an entire society. Awareness of the story or stories in which a moral view, concept, or theory is embedded is necessary if they are to be intelligible. Where this is not recognized, moral concepts may seem to be abstract and ahistorical. Moreover, metaethical theories that naively hypostatize usages of moral language specific to particular and often parochial 'communities' (e.g., the Senior Fellows Common Room) are allowed to go unchallenged. The great virtue of MacIntyre's narration of the history of moral philosophy is that it shows us that these assumptions may be challenged and "that moral concepts themselves have a history. To understand this is to be liberated from any false absolutist claims."[12]

Of course, MacIntyre is not the first person to have noticed that there is something odd about modern moral philosophy. In her classic essay on the state of the discipline, G. E. M. Anscombe opines that it is no longer a profitable object for philosophical attention. As she sees it:

> The concepts of obligation and duty—*moral* obligation and *moral* duty, that is to say—and of what is *morally* right and wrong, and of the *moral* sense of 'ought', ought to be jettisoned if that is psychologically possible; because they are survivals, or derivations from survivals, from an earlier conception of ethics which no longer generally survives, and are only harmful without it.[13]

Without the notion of a divine legislator, necessary to give these concepts of obligation substance and point, philosophers must seek (vainly, in Anscombe's estimation) to fill the void with notions like self-legislation, social convention, and social contract. Anscombe is unimpressed by the results of moral theories that ignore the crucial link between a philosophical concept and its conceptual world.

This linkage can be elucidated, according to MacIntyre, only when moral theories are placed in a followable narrative. The metaethical theory of emotivism is a case in point.

"Emotivism is the doctrine that all evaluative judgments and more specifically all moral judgments are nothing but expressions of attitude or feeling, insofar as they are moral or evaluative in character." Thus, moral judgments are not the sort of things that can be true or false, and "all moral disagreement is rationally interminable."[14] It is a theory that has exerted a strong influence on twentieth-century Anglo-American moral philosophy and on the modern intellectual ethos in general. With respect to the latter, it has taken the form of a particular conception of selfhood that MacIntyre calls "the emotivist self."

The emotivist self can have no rational history in its transitions from one state of moral commitment to another. Inner conflicts are for it necessarily *au fond* the confrontation of one contingent arbitrariness by another. It is a self with no given continuities, save those of the body which is its bearer and of the memory which to the best of its ability gathers in its past.[15]

It is "the peculiarly modern self" unconstrained by the "traditional boundaries provided by a social identity and a view of human life as ordered to a given end." And it is uniquely appropriate to the contemporary cultural climate of "bureaucratic individualism" in which it flourishes.[16]

Nevertheless, MacIntyre judges emotivism to be an inadequate theory. Insofar as emotivism purports to give an account of the *meaning* of certain kinds of sentences, it fails to inform us about what it is that makes a particular statement a moral one. Expressions of feeling or attitude are diverse. When MacIntyre asks the emotivist with what kind of feelings or attitudes and what kind of approval the theory deals, the answer can only be "vacuously circular," namely, with "the type of approval expressed by a specifically moral judgment." Emotivism falters because it does not distinguish between "expressions of personal preference and evaluative (including moral) expressions" and therefore overlooks "the way in which utterances of the first kind depend upon who utters them to whom for any reason-giving force they may have, while utterances of the second kind are not similarly dependent for their reason-giving force on the context of utterance."[17]

Having thus undermined emotivism's cogency as a theory of meaning, MacIntyre suggests that there may be significant aspects of emotivism that such criticism overlooks and that can be seen only when the theory is considered in its historical context. Admitting that emotivism has earlier precursors (e.g., Hume), MacIntyre observes that the theory came into its own only "as a response to a set of theories which flourished, especially in England, between 1903 and 1939."[18] In fact, its origin may be traced to Cambridge and the influential view of G. E. Moore. Moore considered "good" to be a simple, indefinable, "non-natural property," the presence of which cannot be adduced, but only intuited. "Right," for Moore, was descriptive of an action that produced the most good of any available alternative. The highest good in Moore's estimation was that produced by "personal affections and aesthetic enjoyments." MacIntyre observes that these three features of Moore's moral theory are logically independent, that the first is "plainly false," and that the second and third are "at the very least highly contentious."[19] Yet, if Moore's ideas were so "obviously defective," how is it that they were so widely heralded?

As MacIntyre tells the story, Moore's contemporary disciples were disposed to find an escape from what they felt to be the burden of "the moral culture of the late nineteenth century." They were ready to embrace an alternative to both Bentham's utilitarianism and Christian morality, but they were not prepared to leap directly into the modern world. "They felt the need to find objective and impersonal justification for rejecting all claims except those of personal intercourse and of the beautiful." Moore's views seemed compatible with their own values and afforded them a sense of security in that a sense of objectivity was preserved. However, with the passing of two or three decades, this felt need for objectivity largely disappeared. Thus, when Moore's pupils, the modern founders of emotivism such as F. P. Ramsey and C. L. Stevenson, launched their theory, they confused "moral utterance at Cambridge (and in other places with a similar inheritance) after 1903 with moral utterance as such, and . . . they therefore presented what was in essentials a correct account of the former as though it were an account of the latter." MacIntyre regards emotivism as "a cogent theory of use rather than a false theory of meaning" that pertains to "those who continue to use moral and other expressions as if they were governed by objective and impersonal criteria when all grasp of any such criteria has been lost."[20]

My purpose in relating this tale has been to illustrate MacIntyre's contention that moral concepts and theories may be fully understood only when they are placed within a historical narrative of moral development or decline. It is sometimes alleged that such historicism inclines toward the genetic fallacy.[21] Is MacIntyre guilty of confusing an explanation of the historical, psychological, and sociological circumstances of a theory's origin with an argument for or against its validity? In this instance, at least, MacIntyre deserves to be acquitted of the charge. Clearly, he employs analytic arguments against emotivism as a theory of meaning. But in doing so, has he compromised his historicist allegiance?

MacIntyre acknowledges that his method is judged heretical by orthodoxies of both analytic philosophy and historicism. Yet he is unrepentant. Rejecting any sharp distinction between philosophical and historical inquiry, MacIntyre thinks both contribute to the *assessment* as well as the understanding of moral theories. "It is in historical encounter that any given point of view establishes or fails to establish its rational superiority relative to its particular rivals in some specific contexts." While techniques of analytic philosophy are often useful and occasionally sufficient to discredit a view, "analytic philosophy can never provide sufficient grounds for the assertion of any positive standpoint in moral philosophy."[22]

In recent decades, moral philosophy has been preoccupied with the debate between prescriptivism and descriptivism. At issue is the relation between the evaluative and descriptive meanings of a moral judgment. Prescriptivists, respecting what they regard as the absolutely unbridgeable logical gap between fact and value, argue that anything whatsoever may be commended. That commendation is "moral" so long as it accedes to the proper logical form; i.e., that its speaker is prepared to universalize his or her judgment. In this view, there are no limits to the content of one's morality. Descriptivists, on the other hand, contend that there are limitations. Universalizability is not the only differentia of a moral judgment. Facts and values are not always disconnected, as prescriptivists maintain. Rather, according to descriptivists, there are some descriptions of things that give us sufficient reason to evaluate them in a particular way; positively or negatively, as the case may be. Thus, our moral judgments are not matters of radically free choice.

Many of the most respected contemporary moral philosophers have championed the cause of one side or the other. At the same time, there are others who have grown impatient with the terms of the debate. While the prescriptivists seem to overstate the agent's freedom in choosing his or her moral commitments, the descriptivists seem to overlook the way in which descriptions are contingent upon systems of normative principles, world-views, and ways of life. Whatever evaluative force may inhere within certain descriptions, the evaluation adheres not to the brute facts, nor even to the "brute facts relative to a particular description" (to adopt Anscombe's language), but rather to the facts as described within some normative framework. Thus, both prescriptivist and descriptivist accounts of moral judgment misplace the value element.[23]

MacIntyre's narrative of the history of moral philosophy since the Enlightenment is the story of various unsuccessful attempts to provide a common, secular, and rationally justifiable basis of morality. A contemporary chapter in this history is the project of several American neo-Kantian moral philosophers, John Rawls, Alan Donagan, Bernard Gert, and Alan Gewirth, all of whom seek to show that any rational person is logically committed to certain moral principles by virtue of his or her rationality alone. MacIntyre is struck by the fact that there is so much intra-scholastic disagreement on the nature of moral rationality and the principles that are supposedly based upon it:

> If those who claim to be able to formulate moral principles on which rational moral agents ought to agree cannot secure agreement on the formulation of those principles from their colleagues who share their basic philosophical purpose and method, there is ... *prima facie* evidence that their project has failed. ... Each of them in his criticism offers testimony to the failure of his colleague's constructions.[24]

The failure of this school of moral theory to establish morality on a common rational foundation is evidenced further by MacIntyre's examination of one of its most recent influential proposals.

Alan Gewirth's *Reason and Morality* employs what its author calls a "dialectically necessary method." The goal is to derive a rational justification for a supreme moral principle as the necessary entailment of the generic features of human action. Gewirth's argument is summarized in the following passage:

> An agent is a person who initiates or controls his behavior through his unforced, informed choice with a view to achieving various purposes; since he wants to fulfill his purposes he regards his freedom and well-being, the necessary conditions of his successful pursuit of purposes, as necessary goods; hence he holds that he has rights to freedom and well-being; to avoid self-contradiction he must hold that he has these generic rights insofar as he is a prospective purposive agent; hence he must admit that all prospective purposive agents have the generic rights; hence he must acknowledge that he ought at least to refrain from interfering with his recipients' freedom and well-being, so that he ought to act in accord with their generic rights as well as his own.[25]

The final prescription constitutes Gewirth's supreme moral principle, "the principle of generic consistency."

The argument proceeds from the claim that purposive human action requires that agents view the necessary conditions for agency (freedom and well-being) as generic goods. On the basis of what Gewirth sees as the conceptual relation between "goods" and "rights," he argues that an agent's

desire not to be interfered with in attaining these "goods" amounts to a
claim that he or she has a "right" to them. But, as Gewirth is careful to
emphasize, this is only a "prudential" right grounded in the agent's self-
interest. However, the agent recognizes that his claim to this right is solely a
function of his or her agency, and of no other feature that might differentiate him or her from others. Thus, logical consistency requires that an agent
be willing to extend these rights to other agents. From this requirement,
Gewirth derives his supreme moral principle: "Act in accord with the
generic rights of your recipients as well as of yourself."

It is important to notice that what was introduced as a "prudential" right
has been transformed into a moral right. I do not see how Gewirth's
argument entitles him to the conclusion he draws. All that he has established is that each agent must admit, on pain of contradiction, that other
agents have the right to voice their prudential-right claims. But that
cannot entail that agents are required (by self-interest and logical consistency alone) to respect or act in accordance with the prudential-right
claims of other agents. Hence, no moral obligation follows directly from
Gewirth's analysis of the generic goods of action.[26]

MacIntyre faults Gewirth's argument for the way in which it posits a
conceptual relation between goods and rights. In his opinion, they are
quite distinct and separate. While making a "right" claim may entail
universalizability, "it is just this property of universalizability that does not
belong to claims about either the possession of or the need or desire for a
good, even a universally necessary good." Furthermore, the introduction
of "rights" requires its own justification "both because it is at this point a
concept quite new to Gewirth's argument and because of the special
character of a right." Unlike goods necessary for agency that are part of the
universal human condition, rights exist only within certain "socially established sets of rules" that are by no means historically or geographically
universal. Where social institutions and practices do not recognize the
concept of rights, "the making of a claim to a right would be like presenting
a check for payment in a social order that lacked the institution of money."[27]
Thus, this attempt to ground morality in rationality fails. Morality, for
MacIntyre, is a variegated social construction.

A LEGACY OF INCOMMENSURABLE FRAGMENTS

From his narration of the history of modern moral philosophy, MacIntyre draws three conclusions. First, various moral theories gain whatever plausibility they may have only when they are regarded, not as fragments, but as historical developments in a coherent narrative. Second, attempts to do moral philosophy without reference to the stories that shape persons' self-understanding and moral views are misguided. Third, in the current intellectual context, moral debates are often interminable and can be expected to remain so.

This interminability he attributes to the fact that the rival moral arguments are incommensurable and there is no apparent rational way to secure agreement. Furthermore, the problem is exacerbated because, paradoxically, the rival arguments "purport to be *impersonal* rational arguments and as such are usually presented in a mode appropriate to that impersonality." MacIntyre explains that "the different conceptually incommensurable premises of the rival arguments deployed in these debates have a wide variety of historical origins."[28] But the contemporary appeals to rights, universalizability, and natural law often do not acknowledge their conceptual dependence on the views of Locke, Kant, and Aquinas.[29] Each claiming the imprimatur of reason, they simply knock heads over and over again in a debate that no one can win.

This situation must be distinguished, according to MacIntyre, from "moral pluralism" if that is taken to mean "an ordered dialogue of intersecting viewpoints." In contrast, current discussion is often nothing other than "an unharmonious melange of ill-assorted fragments." These fragments are feeble survivals from coherent views of the distant past:

> All those various concepts which inform our moral discourse were originally at home in larger totalities of theory and practice in which they enjoyed a role and function supplied by the contexts of which they have now been deprived. Moreover the concepts we employ have in at least some cases changed their character in the past three hundred years; the evaluative expressions we now use have changed their meaning.[30]

Each concept or argument lacks the power to win agreement. The discussion as a whole is disordered because there is no single, commonly acknowledged conceptual framework or tradition in which it might be conducted.

Contemporary debates about justice in the United States illustrate the incommensurability of rival arguments. Even though the discussion is generally carried on within the fairly narrow parameters of liberal social and political thought, the issues that stand between, say, a Rawls and a Nozick are, in principle, unsettleable. One gives priority to equality of needs, and the other to entitlements. As a result, their claims go past each other and never really engage. MacIntyre thinks this situation obtains, not only among philosophers, but within society as a whole. In our society and others like it, he declares, there can be no hope of moral consensus. "Modern politics is civil war carried on by other means."[31] Thus, the role of the Supreme Court is not to invoke and apply a set of consistent constitutional principles so much as it is to "keep the peace between rival social groups adhering to rival and incompatible principles of justice by displaying a fairness which consists in even-handedness in its adjudications."[32] Of course, even if such efforts succeed in keeping the tactics of this war civil, they do nothing to mend the torn fabric of moral discourse.[33]

Can moral philosophy find a way to break out of this impasse? Believing as he does that all past and present versions of the Enlightenment project to justify morality by reason alone have failed, MacIntyre poses a stark alternative. Either one must accept Nietzsche's diagnosis of the modern predicament or hold that the Enlightenment project was not only ill-fated but unnecessary. MacIntyre opts for the latter. In his opinion, the Aristotelian conception of virtue was not given its due. To be sure, it stood in need of correction in regard to such things as its metaphysical biology, but it was substantially sound. Therefore, MacIntyre endeavors to trace the story of this tradition through its long history for the purpose of resurrecting an account of the virtues as a viable morality in the modern world. His constructive proposal and its problems will be examined in Chapter 4.

3

NARRATIVE AND MORAL CONCEPTS

Stories shape our self-understanding and allow us to make sense of history. In the preceding chapter, I explored a historicist account of moral theory. Now I wish to survey some other and different attempts to interpret moral concepts through narrative and related notions. The philosophers whose views I discuss here are heterogeneous. They do not represent a single school of thought, nor do they all focus on narrative, or story. My purpose is to show, in turn, how narrative may be related to the moral concepts of social groups and individuals. Following some initial exposition, I shall examine three important issues that arise from this literature. Do claims concerning narrative compromise the freedom of moral agents? Does a narrative model of morality allow for the existence of moral rules? Does a narrative model of morality entail relativism and, if so, what kind? These issues will reemerge in Chapter 7 when I consider the adequacy of a narrative-based theological ethic.

THE COMMUNAL CONTEXT OF
MORAL PRACTICES

In Chapter 2, I alluded to the prescriptivist-descriptivist controversy and observed that, in Alasdair MacIntyre's estimation, neither theory is fully adequate. D. Z. Phillips, H. O. Mounce, and R. W. Beardsmore are three philosophers deeply indebted to Wittgenstein who concur in this judgment. They believe that descriptivists (e.g., Philippa Foot) err when they assert that certain facts of human nature entail particular moral judgments and that *apparent* moral disagreements can be resolved by reference to these facts. At the same time, they consider prescriptivists (e.g., R. M. Hare) to be mistaken in severing all connection between fact and value and in permitting any value decision an individual may make to count as moral. Phillips, Mounce, and Beardsmore believe that morality is more diverse than descriptivism allows, but that it is not completely open-ended, as prescriptivism suggests. Their projects seek to chart a middle course between these two theories.

Phillips, Mounce, and Beardsmore maintain that

> in order to make a moral judgment one must belong or be related to a moral practice within which, quite independently of any *decision* on the part of those who belong to that practice, certain facts entail that some things are right or wrong. For those who belong to a moral practice there must be certain occasions on which there is no gap between fact and value.[1]

At the same time, they reject the claim that "a factual statement must entail the same conclusion for every moral agent, irrespective of the moral practices to which he belongs."[2] Thus, limitations on the content of moral judgments are imposed by moral practices, and moral practices are plural and diverse. Moralities must be viewed as systems of communal valuation and practice, or, to use Beardsmore's term, ways of life set within traditions.

In order to illustrate what they mean by a "moral practice," Phillips and Mounce consider the question of how a moral judgment may be justified or rendered intelligible. They argue that it is only because it is generally understood or agreed within our society "that a man should tell the truth rather than lie, respect life rather than kill, [and] be generous rather than mean, [that] it is possible for a man on a particular occasion to make a moral judgment or adopt a moral position."[3] The statement "Lying is wrong," in their view, is not so much a genuine moral judgment as it is a "grammatical remark" concerning the proper use of the word "wrong." By growing up in a society where this is understood and taught, we learn to employ this grammar in making more synthetic moral judgments like "Capital punishment is wrong." According to Beardsmore, "there is a range of concepts (murder, adultery, suicide, truth-telling, etc.) which are in some sense constitutive of a morality. . . . They enable us to recognize a justification as a moral justification and they do so conclusively, for they indicate a person's whole moral outlook."[4] "Moral practice" refers to this kind of communal consensus.

If "Lying is wrong" and "Keeping promises is right" are necessarily true as grammatical rules within a certain moral practice, it is idle to seek any further justification for them. Phillips and Mounce reject the notion that they are observed because they lead to happiness, are conducive to social cohesion, or are reducible in terms of some single "good." These moral rules and concepts are primitive in the sense that there is nothing behind them other than, perhaps, the fact that they are implicit in the idea of society itself.[5]

Moral practices also exist at higher, more complex levels of discourse. There they serve to explain why moral disputes can result in deadlock. Phillips and Mounce imagine an argument between a "scientific rationalist" and a "Roman Catholic housewife" over birth control. The rationalist points to the harm that results from having too many children, and the housewife stresses a mother's honor in participating in the creation of new life. Are there any "facts of human good and harm" that one or the other party overlooks? Might they eventually come to agree on an inclusive list? Phillips and Mounce think not. To be sure, both understand facts about health risks to the mother, economic costs of child-rearing, and over-population. However, for the religious woman, these considerations (though significant) are not decisive. To her mind, the honor of motherhood, the creation of new life, and submission to the will of God are invaluable considerations. She could concur with the rationalist's description of the case only by renouncing her most cherished beliefs. Phillips and Mounce conclude:

> There is no settling of the issue in terms of some supposed common evidence called human good and harm, since what they differ over is precisely the question of what constitutes human good and harm. . . . Their arguments are rooted in different moral traditions within which there are rules for what can and cannot be said.[6]

Debates on abortion, war, justice, and any number of other issues could be used to illustrate the prospect for fundamental moral disagreement.

Several questions regarding the possibilities of appraising a moral practice or tradition—one's own or another's—appear in connection with this example. Can we step back from our traditional commitments and submit them to criticism or exchange them for others? Is it possible even to understand a tradition or practice of which we are not members? Is there some neutral vantage point from which any and all traditions may be assessed critically? Or can it meaningfully be said that some practices are better than others? Phillips, Mounce, and Beardsmore make helpful observations regarding these questions, but I shall postpone my discussion of them until later in this chapter, when the issue of relativism will be addressed more comprehensively.

Phillips, Mounce, and Beardsmore emphasize the social nature of moral concepts and the communal context of their use. Other contemporary moral philosophers focus on individuals and their possibly distinctive understandings and uses of moral concepts. While narrative, or story, is not mentioned by Phillips, Mounce, or Beardsmore, it does receive attention from R. B. Braithwaite, R. W. Hepburn, and Iris Murdoch, three philosophers who examine the moral views of individual agents. I now turn to these discussions.

THE STORIES OF INDIVIDUAL AGENTS

In his Eddington Lecture, "An Empiricist's View of the Nature of Religious Belief," Braithwaite forsakes the classical verificationist doctrine that the meaning of a statement is a function of the process by which it can be verified in order to follow the later Wittgenstein's dictum that meaning is given by the way in which a statement is used. While Braithwaite's theory of ethics is non-propositional, he rejects emotivism. Although emotivists may be correct in thinking that some feeling of approbation accompanies the contemplation of an action held to be right, they are wrong in thinking this attitude to be fundamental. What is fundamental in Braithwaite's "conative" theory is the moral agent's subscription to a policy of action: a declaration of an intention to act, to the best of his or her ability, in accordance with a particular policy.[7]

The superiority of this view is manifest in the answer it affords to the question "What is the reason for my doing what I think I ought to do?" According to Braithwaite, "On every other ethical view there will be a mysterious gap to be filled somehow between the moral judgment and the intention to act in accordance with it: there is no gap if the primary use of a moral assertion is to declare such an intention."[8] Braithwaite believes his analysis is true both to the actual use of moral language and to the spirit of empiricism.

He goes on to suggest that this model also illuminates the meaning of religious assertions. Religious assertions are not merely expressions of primitive feelings; nor are they primarily propositional claims of dogma. Braithwaite says that "the intention of a Christian to follow a Christian way of life is not only the criterion for the sincerity of his belief in the assertions of Christianity; it is the criterion for the meaningfulness of his assertions."[9] The believer's intention to behave in certain ways is constitutive of religious conviction.

Entire systems of religious assertions, therefore, have a moral function, although they are not simply identical to various moralities. There are significant differences. The behavior policy associated with religious assertions is not attached to a single assertion so much as it is embedded within a system of religious assertions. Furthermore, the action guidance of a religious tradition is often conveyed in concrete examples (e.g., the parable of the good Samaritan), rather than by abstract principles such as "Treat yourself and other persons as ends and never as means only." Finally, religious systems typically concern themselves with the believer's inner dispositions, as well as with his or her external actions, in a way that moralities generally do not. Thus, Braithwaite thinks religious assertions can be distinguished from moral ones.

At the same time, he observes that he may have undermined the possibility of distinguishing one religious system from another. If the meaning of each is to be found in its behavior policy, how is one to reply to those who say that Judaism and Christianity (or Buddhism, for that matter) commend the very same life of love? It is Braithwaite's conviction "that there must be some more important difference between an agapeistically policied Christian and an agapeistically policied Jew than that the former attends a church and the latter a synagogue." The salient difference is to be found, according to Braithwaite, in the distinctive stories of the various religious traditions. For his purpose, stories are understood to be "a proposition or a set of propositions which are straightforwardly empirical propositions capable of empirical test and which are thought of by the religious man in connection with his resolution to follow the way of life advocated by his religion."[10] Thus, Christian and Buddhist assertions may be distinguished even where there may appear to be a high degree of similarity in the behavior policies enjoined. A second consequence of this conception of stories is that it allows religious and moral assertions to be

further differentiated. While both religious and moral assertions are decla-
rations of intention to act in certain ways, religious assertions also contain a
propositional element in that they refer to stories.

However, it is propositional in a peculiar sense:

> The reference to the story is not an assertion of the story taken as a
> matter of empirical fact; it is a telling of the story, or an alluding to
> the story, in the way in which one can tell, or allude to, the story of
> a novel with which one is acquainted. To assert the whole set of
> assertions of the Christian religion is both to tell the Christian
> doctrinal story and to confess allegiance to the Christian way of
> life.[11]

Of course, believers tell the story or stories in different ways, and interpretations of the "empirical story-statements" may vary. Indeed, an individual
may hold within his or her set of religious assertions interpretations that
are internally inconsistent. But this is non-problematic, because it is not
necessary for believers to think these assertions actually correspond to
empirical fact. "What is necessary is that the story should be entertained in
thought, i.e., that the statement of the story should be understood as
having a meaning."[12] This meaning is said to be independent of the
empirical truth or falsity of the story's proposition. In fact, Braithwaite
chooses the neutral word "story" from similar terms like "parable," "allegory,"
"fable," "tale," and "myth" precisely because it implies "neither that the
story is believed nor that it is disbelieved."[13]

According to Braithwaite, the relation between "entertaining a story in
thought" and resolving to pursue a specific behavior policy is "a psychological and causal one." Human behavior is a function, not only of propositions one believes to be true, but also of one's wishes, imaginations, and
fantasies. Furthermore, it is widely recognized that fictions such as Bunyan's
Pilgrim's Progress and the novels of Dostoevsky have exerted a strong
influence on the moral and religious lives of Christians. Braithwaite regards
it as an empirical psychological fact "that many people find it easier to
resolve upon and to carry through a course of action which is contrary to
their natural inclinations if this policy is associated in their minds with
certain stories."[14] Thus, the role of story is simply to acknowledge pain and
suffering and to facilitate the doing of good with ease and pleasure.

The psychological function of stories is illustrated in Braithwaite's brief
treatment of the classical question "Is something right because God wills

it, or does God will it because it is right?" Braithwaite observes that "all the moral theistic religions" contain a story to the effect that in following their particular behavior policy an agent does the will of God. However, he does not think that this establishes any intrinsic connection (beyond the psychological causal one) between the story and the conduct. Braithwaite claims that even a simple believer who thinks there actually is a divine commander does His will, not because it is commanded, but rather because it accords with his own moral judgment. The agent's basic commitment to a behavior policy is simply redescribed, insofar as he or she is religious, as doing the will of God. "In religious conviction the resolution to follow a way of life is primary; it is not derived from believing, still less from thinking of, any empirical story. The story may psychologically support the resolution, but it does not logically justify it."[15] Thus, it is evident that, for Braithwaite, stories play only a marginal and supporting role. A person who is sophisticated in moral philosophy and strong of will could dispense with them altogether. Stories do not inform religious persons of anything that could not otherwise be known.

Braithwaite's position is that of a prescriptivist who has an uncharacteristic appreciation for the psychological function of stories. He shares the prescriptivists' common contention that moral and religious commitments are purely subjective and that discussion about these matters can be nothing other than "the exchange of autobiographies." However, Braithwaite believes that something more may be said. Since we are "social animals" who sometimes happen to share "basic wants," we may be able to "pass on information that might prove useful" to another who is "trying to follow a similar way of life."[16] Even where persons are pursuing radically different behavior policies, they may be able to discuss rationally the practical consequences of their chosen ways of life. In this way they can check each other by asking, "Is this really what you wish to bring about?" Of course, if each person in the discussion, upon reflection, replies affirmatively, then nothing more can be said. The rival policies would seem incommensurable and disagreement interminable. It is worth noting that Braithwaite could not attribute this breakdown of conversation (as MacIntyre might) to the fact that the parties are influenced by discrepant stories. Rather, it must be seen as the consequence of his view of policy commitments.

As we have seen, Braithwaite employs the category "story" as a way of accounting for motivation within a thoroughgoing prescriptivism. Other moral philosophers use "story" more broadly. Not merely a psychological crutch, story is, for them, an alternative to the prescriptivists' concentration on decision, principles, and rules. I shall now turn to the 1966 exchange between Hepburn and Murdoch, published under the title "Vision and Choice in Morality." Both are critical (to different degrees) of the exclusive focus on decision, although, as we shall see, they do not follow Phillips, Mounce, and Beardsmore into an analysis of the role of social practices and traditions.

Discussion of the "rule-obedience model" of morality, in Hepburn's judgment, has tended to drown out the testimonies of certain "morally sensitive people . . . who see moral endeavor as the realizing of a pattern of life or the following out of a pilgrimage."[17] The goal, in the terminology of Edwin Muir, is to transmute the external events of one's life story into a "fable" —

> a slowly developing, often elusive, cluster of personal symbols, compounded with childhood memories, foci of aspiration, discoveries in literature, with reference to which [one's] whole life is orientated, and [one's] autobiography knitted into a natural unity, a unity different from any conventional articulation into a life's phases.[18]

The discovery or achievement of this pattern or fable is the task of self-understanding, which must precede any decision on a behavior policy or even a serious posing of the question "What am I to do?"

Sometimes it is maintained that fable is the product of a highly self-conscious labor in which the moral agent is related to his life-pattern as an artist to her artifact. While this analogy is susceptible to egregious overstatement, Hepburn believes that it captures some important features of our moral experience. Wary of the naive pretensions that our fablemaking is a *creatio ex nihilo*, independent of any psychological or environmental determinations, and that our most basic value commitments are consciously and freely chosen, Hepburn locates our artistic freedom in the fact that "it is very much up to a moral agent how he fashions his character by the culture of his imagination, by contemplation of the noble or debased; and the parables, symbols of ideas and concatenations of these which [he calls] 'fables' may clearly play a large part in this."[19] The recalcitrance of the raw material and the intractability of common moral problems require imagination and creativity to be at work in the process whereby the "givens" of existence are woven into an intelligible, coherent pattern. The goal is a unified self capable of embracing past, present, and future. When this is not achieved, one is left with loose ends that lie about one's consciousness "like a heap of dull immovable rubbish" (Edwin Muir).

While Hepburn contends that all persons, or at least all "morally sensitive" persons, engage in this enterprise, he believes that it is "most clearly" exemplified in the moral lives of religious persons. The religious have a special fund of stories and symbols upon which to draw in shaping their moral lives.

> The religious person has his vision of the good life, to the attainment of which all activity is subordinated. All the teachings and actions of the central figure of the religion are charged with the high solemnity and authority of his person. The solemnity is carried back into the believer's conception of what he is doing in performing the humblest moral action; whatever it is, it finds its "position" in the pilgrimage, its solemnizing context in the "fable" of that religion.[20]

It should be observed that this is not simply a restatement of Braithwaite's claim regarding story. Unlike Braithwaite, Hepburn emphasizes the significance of an authoritative figure. Furthermore, Hepburn is not content to confine story's role to its psychological function. He suggests that this "characteristically religious mode of moral teaching" may provide new content:

> In parable . . . a whole slice of life is presented, not an isolated maxim; and the effects of the prescribed conduct (often too the effects of its omission) may be built into the one economical story. In meditation, the believer disciplines his imagination, so as to bring into alignment his own unique conception of his life and the *public* fable of his faith.[21]

Here, the unique content of the religious fable seems to exert authority over the composition of the individual's personal life.

For all his appreciation of the role of story, Hepburn is aware that fables can be solipsistic, self-deceptive, manipulative, and, ultimately, destructive. Therefore, he is concerned to be able to appraise particular fables from a moral point of view. The criteria by which they are to be assessed include coherence, comprehensiveness, and the quality of being "personally vivid."

Of course, these criteria are non-moral. It is not difficult to imagine fables that could pass these non-moral tests, but that, nevertheless, would be highly objectionable. For this reason, Hepburn adds a fourth criterion: a fable should "back up, not fight against, the value-decisions of the person concerned; so that duty does not appear to demand a violating of the pattern, a stepping outside the fable."[22] In light of Hepburn's claim that fables shape personal values, it must be asked whether this fourth criterion really affords the possibility of genuine moral appraisal.

It is clear that Hepburn wants fables to come under "moral criticism and control." This criticism can be in the form of evaluating a fable by means of principles or rules, or it can be expressed by one fable qualifying another. Hepburn says that "to undertake moral control does not *necessarily* mean stepping quite outside the language of 'pattern' into what would then appear as the more fundamental language of 'rule'."[23] But if this is so, then where is the fulcrum upon which one gets critical leverage?

Apparently Hepburn locates it within the fable itself or, more specifically, within the fable's necessary logical form: "If a story is entertained as a parable, it is seen not as a set of events which happened in the past, not as facts about the world, but as a commendation of a universalizable" judgment to the point of saying, "If I were a Jew, then I should be killed."[24]

Even though Hepburn requires his fables to commend a "universalizable programme," he remains wary of what he sees as the dangers of fable-morality. As a defense, he offers three "provisos." First, it must be remembered that fables presuppose "a total way of life" and are not to be equated with the expression of a single maxim. Second, he thinks it perilous to concentrate on agency and character to the exclusion of "the most sober calculation of consequences" of actions. Both must be foci of attention in an adequate morality. Finally, he warns that those who think in terms of fables, especially public religious fables, have more difficulty than do followers of principles in altering their moral judgments to fit new circumstances: "There is great pressure on the fable-follower not to violate the unity of his pattern—a pressure that may readily tempt him away from moral integrity; he meets also the problem (intractable to all but the imaginatively inventive) of how to sew new evaluation to the old fabric."[25] Whether fable-followers actually are at risk to a greater degree than those who are committed to principles is open to question. Nonetheless, Hepburn has noted some significant problems attendant to moralities of story. His warnings show that by no means is he prepared to follow MacIntyre into historicism. Prescriptivist commitments are not abrogated in Hepburn's proposal.

In her contribution to "Vision and Choice in Morality," Iris Murdoch shares Hepburn's dissatisfaction with what she calls "the current view" of morality that focuses on choice of principles, action, and argument. Appreciative though she is of Hepburn's inclusion of fable, she maintains that he does not follow the implications of his argument far enough. As a result, he fails to see the genuine conflict between fables and more rationalistic conceptions of morality. Her own account of "vision" is far more radical than the views of Braithwaite or Hepburn and has wide implications for the morality of stories.

According to Murdoch, Hepburn errs in thinking the phenomenon he identifies to be limited to certain "morally creative" individuals. She suggests that he drop his arbitrary and restrictive insistence that fables be highly coherent and comprehensive:

> If we drop the insistence that fables must be highly coherent and comprehensive, is not fable-making a fairly natural and ordinary activity of human beings and is it not fairly continuous with our most everyday methods of reflecting on and understanding our lives? Here one may distinguish a number of different but similar things which merge into each other. There is the highly reflective and imaginative personal fable (which Mr. Hepburn mainly has in mind), the "story of one's life," of which, whether kept privately or displayed to others, most people have formed some conception, more ephemeral and disconnected stories and shapings of particular incidents or periods, metaphors explanatory of situations or changes, miscellaneous personal attitudes or visions which may show dramatically in special modes of description or in a more diffused manner in the selection of explanatory concepts. This indicates . . . a region in which the "personal visions" in question may be overt or secret, more or less pictorial, and in the ordinary sense of the word, imaginative or unimaginative. This is the variegated region to which we must attend.[26]

While the reigning school of moral philosophy tends to view these "personal visions" as irrelevant or tangential to morality, Murdoch regards them as "direct expressions of a person's 'moral nature' or 'moral being' [which demand] a type of description which is not limited to the choice and argument model."[27]

For her, differences between moral positions are not merely the result of discrepant choices or value commitments. Moral differences are conceptual and reflect differences in vision: "A moral concept seems less like a movable and extensible ring laid down to cover a certain area of fact, and more like a total difference of *Gestalt*; we differ not only because we select different objects out of the same world but because we see different worlds." Because there are no neutral descriptions of the facts, it is not to be expected that observers will concur about what they see. Communication of a new moral concept "may involve the communication of a completely new, possibly far-reaching and coherent, vision." Obviously, this is not easy to achieve. Thus, she concludes, "we cannot always *understand* other people's moral concepts."[28]

Murdoch understands that the view of morality she sketches has implications that set it at odds with recent moral philosophy. In the face of widespread insistence that "fact" and "value" be kept radically distinct and separate, Murdoch boldly argues that they "merge in a quite innocuous way." While she shares non-naturalism's suspicion of claims for the existence of metaphysical entities, she rejects its dogma that moral terms have meaning "via movable specification of empirical criteria, plus recommendation." If, as she maintains, moral differences are differences of vision rather than choice, "then the prohibition on defining value in terms of fact loses much of its point." It may continue to serve some purpose — a normative, liberal purpose — in that it mandates respect for others' views, readiness to question one's own position, and willingness to engage in reflective argument. But the violation of the prohibition, the merging of fact and value, no longer may be considered a *philosophical* error. "If moral concepts are regarded as deep moral configurations of the world, rather than as lines drawn round separable factual areas, then there will be no facts 'behind them' for them to be erroneously defined in terms of."[29] Thus, if Murdoch is right, the philosophical "problem" of the relation between "fact" and "value" must be construed in a new and different way.

Similarly revisionistic is Murdoch's reluctance to stipulate a single logical form for what is, in fact, "complex and various." For example, she thinks it a mistake for Hepburn to insist that moral (in the generic sense) fables include or imply universalizable rules. While it may be true that fables that express "some sort of generally accepted and comprehensible social pattern" (such as those of the major religious traditions) have practical implications that *can* be regarded as universal rules, Murdoch envisions other fables that do not. The more individually personalized a fable is, the less amenable it is to universalization. If the person who entertains the fable imagines himself or herself to be unique in terms of status or destiny, it is idle to require him or her to agree that anyone similarly circumstanced should act as he or she does. No one else could be in requisitely similar circumstances. As Murdoch says, "If one is Napoleon one does not think that everyone should do as one does oneself." Are we, then, to deny that such an individual can make moral judgments? Murdoch finds such a denial to be pointless. The individual's attitude, judgment, and conduct may be praiseworthy or blameworthy, but certainly it is generically moral. Certain idealist, existentialist, and even Roman Catholic conceptions of morality seem to her to be "unconnected with the view that morality is essentially universal rules."[30]

Murdoch emphasizes the importance of seeing other persons as they are, not as we want or imagine them to be. She believes that

> philosophers have been misled, not only by a rationalistic desire for unity, but also by certain simplified and generalized moral attitudes current in our society, into seeking a single philosophical definition of morality. If, however, we go back again to the data we see that there are fundamentally different moral pictures which different individuals use or which the same individual may use at different times. . . . For purposes of analysis moral philosophy should remain at the level of the differences, taking the moral forms of life as given, and not try to *get behind them* to a single form.[31]

From the suggestion that philosophers ought to attend to the particularities and differences within contemporary society, it would seem to follow that they also should be sensitive to the diversity of moral conceptualities of the past. This conclusion is evidenced by Murdoch's statement that "morality must, to some extent at any rate, be studied historically."[32] I take this methodological proposal to be a third implication of her conception of morality.

The fourth controversial implication of Murdoch's account concerns human freedom. In what she takes to be the dominant school of thought in moral philosophy, agents are supposed to survey the neutral facts and then exercise their radical freedom of choice. "If, however, we hold that a man's morality is not only his choices but his vision, then this may be deep, ramified, hard to change, and not easily open to argument." The price of Murdoch's realism in this regard is a diminution of freedom, but she is not deterred. There is, in her estimation, "no need to equate the freedom needed to ensure morality with a complete independence of deep conceptual attitudes." For her, freedom consists in the ability to "deepen" and "reorganize" our concepts or to exchange one for another. "Moral freedom looks more like a mode of reflection which we may have to achieve, and less like a capacity to vary our choices which we have by definition."[33] She sees in this no disadvantage, and, in any case, it does not succumb to mistaking a wish for a fact. Later, we shall have occasion to recall how this view of freedom places constraints upon an ethic of character shaped by story, or narrative.

In the remainder of this chapter, I want to return to three broad issues already identified: the kind or degree of freedom an agent may have in relation to the stories of his or her tradition, the place of universal rules within a narrative model of morality, and the sort of relativism these accounts may entail. Each of these is equally relevant to uses of narrative in theological ethics and will be discussed in that context in Chapter 7. I shall begin with the first.

FREEDOM AND AGENCY

The issue of freedom can be approached in several ways. First, it may be asked whether narratives in their intrinsic form depict human agency in such a way that the freedom of their characters is restricted. If characters are simply pushed and pulled about by the necessities of authorial design, and if we are to fit ourselves into one of the narrative "types," it might seem that there is little room for freedom within a narrative morality. Of course, the degree to which the thoughts and actions of characters seem forced varies. We often say that in a good story the characters do not seem to be pawns moved to suit the author's purposes. Rather, they seem to have lives of their own.

It has been argued that a certain kind of narrative (what Hans Frei, following Erich Auerbach, calls "realistic narrative") is highly appropriate for displaying the kind of freedom persons do, in fact, have. Narratives of this sort present agency as a dialectical relation between intention and circumstance. Characters project their intentions into the world, and circumstances conspire to limit the possibility of carrying them out. Things happen to characters in certain ways, but they are not thereby prevented from intending new actions that are uniquely their own. Who they are and what happens to them form an ongoing system of interactions that allows the characters a measure of freedom in that they are neither determined entirely nor prevented from having their own intentions.[34]

If narrative form itself does not necessarily eliminate agency, is our appropriation of stories an imitative exercise in which we are more bound than free? One reply is to say that when we acknowledge the influence stories exert on us and recognize ourselves in relation to the narrative "types," we are not simply copying the characters or attempting to repeat their actions. As Murdoch says, narratives offer a rich assortment of images, metaphors, concepts, and characters. When we appropriate the story for ourselves, we select from this assortment and reassemble the parts in an individualized way. A narrative or a tradition, especially one as diverse as, for example, Christian scripture, provides resources for a wide variety of construals or retellings, as we shall see in subsequent chapters. These choices are expressions of one sort of freedom in relation to the various features of a given narrative.

Nevertheless, one may ask about our freedom over against the narrative as a whole. If it is the case that our self-understanding, our worldview, and our morality are influenced profoundly by the narrative or narratives to which we are related, is our freedom as moral agents thereby restricted or removed entirely? Clearly, the way in which Braithwaite envisions stories poses no such threat to human freedom. We may pick and choose from a variety of stories, or we may dispense with stories altogether, relying instead on our commitment to certain moral principles. Murdoch's depiction of morality, on the other hand, allows little room for choice. In her view, stories seem to capture us, bewitching our vision in such a way that we can apprehend only what our story allows. To some extent, this may represent "overcompensation" for the kind of freedom posited by choice- or decision-oriented theories of morality. Nevertheless, it is overstatement. As Gene Outka observes, narratives do not embrace us so tightly that we cannot withhold our assent from the roles they bequeath to us. While we cannot escape "coming to terms" with the stories of our childhood, family, and tradition, we can decline to identify with all or part of this heritage.[35]

The sociologist Peter Berger has likened the human world to a puppet theater in which persons play their roles suspended from subtle strings pulled about according to the logic of the theater:

> For a moment we see ourselves as puppets indeed. But then we grasp a decisive difference between the puppet theater and our own drama. Unlike the puppets, we have the possibility of stopping our movements, looking up and perceiving the machinery by which we have been moved. In this fact lie the first steps toward freedom.[36]

Translating the metaphor from drama to narrative, it could be said that, however much our stories shape our dispositions and our vision, it is possible for us to be conscious of that influence. Once it is perceived, it may be affirmed or resisted. Although some proponents of story seem to be of mixed mind about our potential for self-awareness and change, it seems to me that this capacity is essential to a conception of freedom strong enough to bear the weight of a notion of moral responsibility.

Is perceiving the "strings" by which stories exert their influence a sufficient (as well as a necessary) condition for asserting our freedom? Or is it the case that in order to be free we must be able to reach up and cut the strings? It is not necessary to posit the capacity to sever the connections to any and all narratives in order to preserve freedom.

Persons are free to affirm or deny their desires and motivations however they may have come to be the way they are. In self-evaluation they can judge some of their dispositions to be superior to others. They are capable of wanting to be different than they are. This is true even when the capacity actually to change themselves may be minimal or nonexistent. Such a conception of relative freedom to assent to or resist determining influences (including those of stories) is sufficiently robust to undergird moral responsibility.[37]

As we have seen, some of those who base morality upon narrative maintain that persons are free to reject or alter their tradition. Beardsmore, for example, recognizes that there have been moral revolutionaries or rebels, like Nietzsche, Kierkegaard, Marx, Tolstoy, or Christ, who sought to overturn, or at least amend, the values of their society. Nevertheless, he warns that it is a mistake to think that "the views of the revolutionary have no points of contact with other moralities, nor even that they have no points of contact with the moral position that he is rejecting." Were there no continuities whatsoever, the rebel's views would be unintelligible even to himself. However revisionary a proposal may be, "it can be seen to have connections with a tradition which encompasses both what he accepts and what he rejects."[38] Only a maniac could completely disregard all aspects of her tradition simultaneously, and the result would be that she could not understand her "new" morality. While even the revolutionary must begin somewhere, i.e., in a narrative or tradition, the freedom he or she retains over against a tradition or story and his or her capacity to change or reject it are both substantial and complex.[39]

STORIES AND RULES

The second issue arising from these discussions is the relation between narrative and rules. With the exception of Braithwaite, all of the proponents of story, vision, and virtue we have considered reject the idea that morality is primarily a matter of identifying, applying, and obeying principles or rules. MacIntyre, as we have seen, undermines Gewirth's attempt to generate universal principles from an account of reason and agency. Nevertheless, as MacIntyre himself acknowledges, it is not easy to give up the conviction that rules are of some fundamental importance. Alan Donagan, another neo-Kantian, has what is to my mind a persuasive reply to those who see in rules nothing but empty formalism. He is unwilling to concede the superiority of a morality of "conformity to the mores of an actual ethical community" (what Hegel called *Sittlichkeit*) over one of obedience to "a law binding upon all rational creatures by virtue of their rationality" (*die Moralität*).[40]

Donagan tells the story of an Austrian Roman Catholic farmer who refused induction into the German army in 1943 because he judged the war his country was waging to be unjust. Both his parish priest and his bishop urged him to change his mind on the grounds that an uneducated farmer was in no position to make an informed judgment about the justice of the war. But the man remained faithful to reason and conscience and was beheaded. Donagan sees in this an example of "the depravation of the *Sittlichkeit* of an ethical community whose members had lost the habit of moral self-criticism." While traditional Catholic moral theory afforded precepts by which one could determine the moral status of that or any other war, the farmer's clergymen embraced the mores of their community to the point of denying that any individual was capable of judging the justice or injustice of the community's war. Here, Donagan concludes, "what is exposed as empty, as lacking specific content, as allowing any filling whatever, is not *Moralität*, but *Sittlichkeit*."[41]

But is Donagan really entitled to his conclusion? A champion of coherentism might interpret the story as representing not a conflict between *Sittlichkeit* and *Moralität* but rather a clash between rival *Sittlichkeiten* in which the unfortunate farmer held membership. Although he is undeniably courageous, the farmer should not be regarded as a paragon of moral rationality (*Moralität*). Such an interpretation is unpersuasive. What the story illustrates is not a church-state conflict or even an intramural disagreement within the church. It is hardly likely that the uneducated farmer rejected the counsel of his religious teachers on the grounds that his construal of the Catholic moral tradition was more authentic than theirs. It is far more plausible to suppose that the farmer simply "knew" gross injustice when he saw it and therefore refused to conform to the mores of his actual religious community as exemplified by its clergy. Thus, Donagan's use of the illustration is vindicated.

In my judgment, Donagan's story suggests two things. First, "foundationalism" in moral theory may not be as bankrupt as "coherentists" like MacIntyre allege. Second, those who approach, if not adopt, coherentism in the course of emphasizing narrative, or story, ought not to despise or reject too readily the role of principles and rules.

Might some other foundationalist attempt to establish universal rules fare better than Gewirth's against criticism from proponents of narrative? It seems to me that Bernard Gert's account of "the moral rules" is such an attempt. To be sure, Gert is not concerned with narrative. However, the rational foundation for morality he provides is not incompatible with appreciation for at least some of the claims made for the role of narrative. Since, as announced at the outset, I want to argue that both rules and narrative are ingredient to a coherent and plausible understanding of morality, it is useful to observe how Gert and another "non-narrativist," P. F. Strawson, conceptualize morality in ways that do not systematically exclude attention to narrative.

Despite the fact that he is numbered among those foundationalists MacIntyre believes to be chasing an illusion, Gert does not maintain that there is, in principle, a single correct answer to every moral question or dilemma. But neither does he agree with R. M. Hare that many moral disagreements are unresolvable. Gert claims only to be able to set limits on moral disagreement by means of his account of rationality. As a self-styled student of Hobbes, Gert makes relatively modest assumptions about what reason requires. A rational person, for Gert, is someone whose desires and beliefs are not irrational. Wanting to be as inclusive as possible, Gert excludes only those desires and beliefs that virtually everyone with sufficient intelligence and experience to be a moral agent would regard as irrational to act upon in the absence of some special justifying reason that all of them would accept. Thus, an irrational belief would be something like "I am immortal," and an irrational desire would be a desire to suffer pain or to be deprived of liberty simply for the experience. Reason requires only the recognition that persons are susceptible to certain specifiable harms. Since all rational persons desire protection from these harms, it is in their self-interest to refrain from inflicting them on others as a means of securing reciprocal restraint on the part of their neighbors.

Gert thinks there is a conceptual or analytic relationship between being rational and having a certain attitude toward a particular set of rules. These rules include such common injunctions as "Don't kill," "Don't cause pain," "Don't deprive others of pleasure, freedom, or opportunity," "Don't deceive," and "Don't break promises." Gert holds that these may be established and justified as "the moral rules" by demonstrating that all rational persons would take the following attitude toward them:

> I want all other people to obey the rule with regard to anyone with whom I am concerned (including myself) except when they have a good specific reason for thinking that either that person or myself (possibly the same) has (or would have if he knew the facts) a rational desire that the rule not be obeyed with regard to him.[42]

Given this desire and the fact that all are susceptible to harm from the violation of the rules, a rational person has an interest in persuading others to adopt this attitude with respect to those for whom he or she cares. Of course, every person cares about a different group of people. Therefore, the only way to achieve universal agreement and common security is for each person to "publicly advocate" universal compliance and punishment for unjustifiable violations. Thus, the justifiable moral rules are those toward which all rational persons would adopt the attitude:

> Everyone is to obey the rule with regard to everyone except when he could publicly advocate violating it. Anyone who violates the rule when he could not publicly advocate such a violation may be punished.[43]

This is what Gert calls "the moral attitude."

While I cannot do justice to the sophistication or complexity of Gert's argument here, this should be enough to suggest both the content of his basic morality and the way in which he thinks it can be justified. The moral rules refer to negative duties and may be summarized as "Don't cause evil." Of course, there is more to morality than refraining from causing evil, but Gert sees no way to secure universal agreement on the content of anything beyond the moral rules. The rules provide a common foundation upon which rational persons are free to build as they deem fit.

Gert calls this second tier the realm of "moral ideals." Moral ideals refer to positive duties that can be summarized as "Prevent evil." Here, rational persons are free to differ as to the stringency, scope, and relative importance of the various ideals. Strictly personal ideals, virtues, and goods also affect how persons will choose to enact moral ideals. The variety is infinite, and Gert has no interest in trying to standardize individual conceptions. While he observes that "all of the major religions of mankind urge their adherents to follow the moral and utilitarian ideals," some religions also advocate the development of certain personality traits and "the ideal of loving kindness, which goes beyond what is encouraged by the moral ideals."[44] So long as persons acknowledge the moral rules that reason requires, they may construct diverse moralities that reflect the myriad policy options that reason allows.

Although Gert is not concerned with explaining how people acquire their conceptions of the moral ideals, there is nothing in his account of morality that would prevent one from attributing it to the influence of particular narratives.[45] Furthermore, there is no reason why non-coherentist proponents of narrative must resist such a moral theory. Of course, Gert's Hobbesian argument may be flawed, and it is not my present purpose to defend it in detail. However, assuming that the argument is defensible, it does not significantly erode many of the claims of narrative theorists. It would mean that morality is not entirely defined by or dependent on narrative (contra coherentism), but, as we have seen, most narrative theories try to incorporate some sort of universal virtues or common agreements anyway. My point is simply that Gert's moral rules are as plausible candidates for the common element as any we have encountered.

A similarly two-tiered moral system has been sketched by P. F. Strawson. "The region of the ethical" he describes as "a region of diverse, certainly incompatible, and possibly practically conflicting ideal images or pictures of a human life, or of human life; and it is a region in which many such incompatible pictures may secure at least the imaginative, though doubtless not often the practical, allegiance of a single person."[46] Not only does

Strawson think this to be descriptively accurate; he also prizes this "evaluative diversity" as a positive contribution to the "human scene." At the same time, Strawson recognizes that "the sphere of morality" is usually explained in terms of "rules or principles governing human behavior which apply universally within a community or class."[47] It is the way in which Strawson conceives the relation between "the ethical" and "the moral" that is of present interest.

What he calls "a minimal interpretation of morality" is said to be prerequisite to any form of social organization: "It is a condition of the existence . . . of any human community that certain expectations of behavior on the part of its members should be pretty regularly fulfilled: that some duties . . . should be performed, some obligations acknowledged, some rules observed." This morality is a "public convenience" without which those aspects of social existence we value most highly would be impossible. Moreover, Strawson holds that "certain human interests are so fundamental and so general that they must be universally acknowledged in some form and to some degree in any conceivable moral community." Thus, despite the diversity of moral systems, he believes it possible to identify "certain general virtues or obligations [which] will be a logically or humanly necessary feature of almost any conceivable moral system."[48] These include some form of honesty and justice, as well as obligations to mutual aid and abstention from injury. He acknowledges that his view places limits on what can count as a moral claim and thus scales down freedom of choice. However, Strawson judges it to be both true to the facts and the basis for the possibility of moral criticism.

How are the various ideal pictures of forms of life related to the minimal interpretation of morality? Strawson says they presuppose it. "The possibility of the pursuit of an ideal form of life quite pragmatically requires membership of a moral community or of moral communities." The demands of each may conflict on occasion or very often. But he also envisions a case in which "it may be that a picture of the ideal life is precisely one in which the interests of morality are dominant, are given an ideal, overriding value." This confirmation of the minimal morality may be total or partial, and he observes that the latter obtains for "that ideal picture in which obedience to the command to love one another appears as the supreme value."[49] Therefore, according to Strawson, ideal pictures of life are not intrinsically hostile to conceptions of moral duties and rules held in common. Furthermore, the Christian form of life, which will be discussed in subsequent chapters, may be especially appreciative of these shared dimensions of morality.

It would be wrong to suggest that the authors surveyed in this chapter are all or similarly hostile to foundationalism or to the admission that morality, at least a part of it, involves rules. Braithwaite and Hepburn clearly acknowledge the status of rules as being independent of narrative. Even Murdoch recognizes that "everyday morality, in our society at any rate, is of the kind . . . where rules are universal, fairly general without being too general, and where clear and aboveboard factual reasoning is required to justify choices." Her point is simply that morality conceived as rules "is an attempt to secure us against the ambiguity of the world," and yet there are times when it is proper to stress (and other types of morality that emphasize) the "incomprehensibility" of the world and of other persons.[50]

It should not be overlooked here that even MacIntyre's constructive proposal, to be discussed in the next chapter, seeks, not to supplant rules, but only to loosen their hegemony over the field of the moral. Despite his historicism and coherentism, MacIntyre agrees with Aristotle that morality consists of both virtues and rules or laws. Nevertheless, MacIntyre seems to concur with those who maintain that while stories—good stories, anyway—include rules, those rules have no independent, foundational status over against the stories that bear them. There can be no point of critical reference outside the realm of stories from which one could survey the entire scene and pick one's story accordingly. His contention is that we cannot make sense of rules if we begin with them. In terms of epistemological priority, it is the narratives that must come first. Only when rules are located within a tradition and its narrative do they become intelligible.[51]

However, even if it is granted that rules can be conveyed meaningfully only through particular stories, one may ask whether rules can be isolated and extracted from a story for the purpose of making judgments about that and other stories and about the world. If there can be no such abstraction and distantiation from particular stories, it would seem that the prospect for moral evaluation is bleak. Of course, historicists can allow for this "abridgment," but they cannot permit the postulation of an independent vantage point. As a result, all stories are on all fours with each other, and it is impossible to "check" any of them against the moral rules. The consequences of this impossibility are immense. In Chapter 7, I shall return to this point in connection with Stanley Hauerwas's theological project.

RELATIVISM

The final issue to be addressed in this chapter is what W. B. Gallie considers the most important question facing contemporary moral philosophy: "One morality or many?"[52] Talk about traditions, practices, stories, and narratives seems to suggest that there are many moralities. Does such talk entail relativism, and, if so, what sort of relativism is it?

To begin, Phillips and Mounce strenuously deny that their view of practices leads either to skepticism or a vicious relativism. It is true, of course, that by emphasizing the social nature of moral conventions and practices they may seem to approach the Protagorean notion that the truth or falsity of moral judgments is determined by agreement of the majority. However, Phillips and Mounce argue that their position is significantly different. They deny that they have in any way precluded the possibility of a moral agent maintaining that she is correct in her judgment and the majority is wrong on any given occasion. One can criticize the moral judgments of one's neighbors (as did Donagan's Austrian farmer) and even the content of practices of which one is not a member. Moral agreement with others is never desired for its own sake without regard for the content of the shared values. Morality, for Phillips and Mounce, never amounts to merely "doing the done thing."

They judge that relativists (and those who fail to distinguish their theory of moral practices from relativism) are guilty of a fundamental error: "Relativists treat moral judgments as if they were statements about certain of the conditions on which they depend for their sense."[53] Although moral judgments can only be made against a background of agreement, they ought not to be identified with that background. As an example, they cite the idea of parental obligation. 'Parental obligation' is meaningful only when it is considered against a certain background, the family. Nevertheless, the feeling of parental obligation is not exclusively, or even primarily, a feeling about the institution of the family. It is, rather, a feeling for a child that arises only against a particular institutional background.

Equally erroneous is the relativists' tendency to reduce the content of moral judgments and values to facts about the agent's biography (the way in which she was reared, educated, or employed) or the historical development of the values in question. "If the expression of moral opinions were simply a way of expressing the circumstances by which these opinions came to be held, moral agreement or disagreement would be impossible given ignorance of such circumstances."[54] Phillips and Mounce think it obvious that this is not the case. Moral disagreement is both possible and genuine even when such knowledge is absent. Moreover, access to the information does not, by itself, resolve the dispute.

Phillips and Mounce recognize "the multiplicity of moral practices" and the possibility that, even within a society, discussions about moral judgments may end in "moral deadlock." This is so because there is no way independently to validate particular moral practices. Unlike theories, moral practices "are not accounts or interpretations of anything more ultimate than themselves."[55] When the parties to a moral disagreement have explored the contested issues and are certain of their respective convictions, it would be odd for one of them to ask, "And who is right?" According to Phillips and Mounce, neither party would yield, nor grant that her "rightness" consisted in nothing other than her saying so. Nor could the matter be settled by some 'ideal observer'. While both parties might be prepared to defer to God's judgment, neither would be in a better position to say what that is, and the discussion would remain deadlocked. Phillips and Mounce contend that the notion of anyone's being in a "better position" to assess which morality is correct is meaningless and confused. There can be no transcendental position from which to judge. The parties can only confess, "These are the values we think important, worth defending and fighting for."[56]

The sort of relativism entailed by the Phillips and Mounce account of moral practices seems pernicious, in their view, only on the mistaken assumption that one can achieve this transcendental vantage point. Once that is given up, the relativistic consequences of Phillips and Mounce's position seem innocuous. Neither of the parties in the aforementioned dispute is thereby required, nor should she be expected, to doubt the truth of her convictions or to say, "We're both right from our different points of view." Moreover, the theory does not foreclose the possibility of generating moral disagreement. There can be discussion between adherents of different moral practices. In fact, Phillips and Mounce expect it, because

> very many people have no such thing as a complete moral code, a systematic morality. More often than not our lives are affected by diverse moral influences. We feel the attraction of different moral views, and may be torn between them. Furthermore, many moral viewpoints develop in relation to one another; there is the thrust and counterthrust of moral warfare, so to speak.[57]

At the same time, they agree with Murdoch that there may be instances when "we should not be afraid to say that we fail to get the feel of a moral problem because it is part of a moral viewpoint so disparate from our own that we fail to find a conceptual foothold which would enable us to understand it."[58]

This failure is most likely to occur when persons consider the moral practices of other cultures. The result of Phillips and Mounce's view is not that every conceivable behavior in another culture must be condoned as "right for them." They simply point out that an effort must be made to understand an action within its own cultural context. For example, they believe that it would be mistaken for us to describe what Abraham was about to do to Isaac on Mount Moriah as child abuse, torture, or attempted murder. Their caution does not follow from some flabby notion of tolerance, but from an attempt to understand the practice of child sacrifice in pre-Abrahamic Hebrew society. When confronted by an equally appalling practice in another, contemporary culture, one is permitted by Phillips and Mounce's view to make an adverse judgment about it once it has been understood. One may even see that a particular act is properly described as "murder" after all, and attempt to prevent it. What Phillips and Mounce insist on is that

> our judgments of these practices must wait on an understanding of them. Whatever our judgments are, they must not distort the nature of the actions judged by ignoring the cultural institutions within which they have their meaning or the relations of ideas involved in the participants' understanding and execution of them.[59]

And that applies as much to judgments about practices within our society as it does to those of other societies. Like Murdoch, Phillips and Mounce are content to explore the differences between moralities or "forms of life," forbearing to try to get behind the variety to a single form.

Assuming that it is impossible to attain a transcendental perspective, and that Phillips and Mounce's account of relativism is both accurate and acceptable, one may require, nevertheless, that a narrative moral theory allow us some critical distance from our stories. In my discussion of freedom, I concluded that this is possible. We can criticize our stories and even exchange them for others. Now the question arises whether some stories may be better than others in this respect. Do some stories allow, invite, or encourage this distantiation more than others? And if they do, does this make them better morally? Several of the authors do attempt to discriminate between stories. Hepburn, it may be recalled, says that fables may be graded on the non-moral bases of their comprehensiveness, coherence, and vividness. He also stipulates that a fable or pattern "must be open to moral claims from without, must be ready to admit its own inadequacy."[60] Where narrative-independent moral principles collide with fables, fables must give way. In light of what he says about the stories of major religions being resistant to emendation, Hepburn would seem to be led to the conclusion that Jewish and Christian stories are *worse* than some fragmentary fable that more readily accedes to its own inadequacy. Of course, if it were the case that Jewish, Christian, or other religious stories were so constituted that collisions with narrative-independent moral principles were rare, then their resistance would make little practical difference.

MacIntyre, too, wishes to establish criteria for the evaluation of stories proffered as answers to what he sees as "the most basic question" for each moral agent: "Of what histories am I a part?" Three requirements (not all of which are moral) for an adequate narrative are identified. First, "only true [non-mythological] stories are acceptable." Second, it must have some "generic shape" and belong to some "identifiable genre." His third requirement is perhaps the most interesting. Any acceptable narrative

> must do justice to the facts of moral complexity and more especially to the tragic character of human existence. This tragic character is inseparable from the relationship of the absolute and unconditional requirements of morality to guilt and evil. It puts the vulnerability and failures of moral agents at the center of the moral picture.[61]

MacIntyre's point here is not dissimilar to Phillips and Mounce's underscoring that it is well to recognize that there are moral points of view other than one's own, and that some moral viewpoints develop only in exchange with others.

That conversation and at least some degree of common agreement among stories are possible is the finding of several of the philosophers under discussion. This "commonality" is accounted for in various ways. Phillips and Mounce (and others influenced by Wittgenstein) regard it as nothing more than a "family resemblance" or a contingent overlapping that, desirable as it may be, is not to be expected in every case. On the other hand, others of those whose views I have surveyed do count on the various stories, traditions, or ideals having at least something in common.

MacIntyre, Gert, and Strawson (to be sure, for different reasons) all maintain that the idea of a society dictates a certain core content, however radically moralities may diverge from one another.

However the possibility of commonality is to be explained, it is welcome. Ours is a pluralistic world whose future prospects may well depend upon our ability and willingness to converse with one another. Where commonality among stories is dismissed or despised, politics may degenerate from "war by other means" (MacIntyre) to war by any means.

To conclude: an adequate comprehensive account of morality must include attention to both narratives and ideals on the one hand, and universal virtues, moral rules, and law on the other. Of course, some narratives may be more worthy of loyalty than others. For instance, stories that encourage internal reflection and criticism, that are willing to engage in conversation with other stories, and that acknowledge, celebrate, and seek to extend whatever commonality they may share might be deemed morally superior to those that do not. But whatever normative judgments might be made, narrative refers to only one aspect of morality. Proposals regarding narrative may be superimposed on common morality as the upper level of a two-tiered system, or they may hold that universal virtues and rules are constituent to all socially viable narratives. What they cannot do is overlook or reject those shared elements that make possible coexistence in pluralistic society and some, though by no means complete, agreement.

4

VIRTUE AND NARRATIVE:
A PHILOSOPHICAL PROPOSAL

Only in the last decade has use of the word "virtue" ceased to be unfashionable. Some of the "comic," "priggish," and "self-deceptive" associations the word acquired have sloughed off, and moral philosophers are returning to this traditional notion.[1] Although not the first to redirect attention to virtue, Alasdair MacIntyre is perhaps the most influential of the recent converts. His constructive proposal for the rehabilitation of an ethic of virtue shaped by narrative, now in an expanded second edition, merits separate consideration in this chapter. Not only has it found a wide audience, by no means restricted to professional philosophers, but it stands as the preeminent contemporary philosophical study of narrative and morality. Moreover, it serves as a worthy counterpart to the narrative theological ethics of Stanley Hauerwas, to be discussed in a later chapter.

From his narrative of the history of moral philosophy, MacIntyre concludes that the Enlightenment project of grounding morality within the limits of reason alone was and remains a failure. The way out of our modern predicament (described in Chapter 2) is to be found in a refurbished but recognizably Aristotelian ethic of virtue. His most prominent renovation is the role he accords narrative.

MacIntyre observes that in Greek, medieval, and Renaissance cultures, "the chief means of moral education is the telling of stories." This was appropriate, in part, because morality did not yet exist in the modern sense of something distinct from social structures. But, more important, this classical perspective was based upon the recognition that "human life has a determinative form, the form of a certain kind of story. It is not just that poems and sagas narrate what happens to men and women, but that in their narrative form poems and sagas capture a form that was already present in the lives which they relate." Narratives and human character stand in a relation of mutual presupposition. Thus, for example, "to understand courage as a virtue is not just to understand how it may be exhibited in character, but also what place it can have in a certain kind of enacted story." Of course, the virtues of pre-Christian Icelandic society are different from those of Athens. But this diversity in the accounts of the virtues is to be expected because the narratives, and the related conceptions of character, are diverse. "Every particular view of the virtues is linked to some particular notion of the narrative structure or structures of human life."[2]

Nevertheless, MacIntyre contends that it is possible to identify "a unitary core concept of the virtues" that links the various moral traditions he explores and undergirds his constructive proposal. This identification takes place in a three-stage process of logical development. Taken together, the stages purport to provide the rationale for MacIntyre's insistence that "the concept of a virtue . . . always requires for its application the acceptance of some prior account of certain features of social and moral life in terms of which it has to be defined and explained."[3]

MacINTYRE'S CONSTRUCTIVE ACCOUNT

At the first stage, MacIntyre says that virtues receive their primary, though not their only, definition within a particular type of "practice." He defines a practice as

> any coherent and complex form of socially established cooperative human activity through which goods internal to that form of activity are realised in the course of trying to achieve those standards of excellence which are appropriate to, and practically definitive of, that form of activity, with the result that human powers to achieve excellence, and human conceptions of the ends and goods involved, are systematically extended.[4]

With this formidable definition, MacIntyre intends to identify as practices such things as "arts, sciences, games, politics in the Aristotelian sense, [and] the making and sustaining of family life."[5]

Practices do for MacIntyre what the notion of a human *telos* did for Aristotle and his successors. They provide a context in which the content of the virtues may be specified. Although for the Greeks and for Aquinas both the *telos* and virtues were underwritten by the cosmic order, for MacIntyre the guarantee must be internal to human activity. While he does not regard a divine sanction as being necessary, he says theists were correct insofar as they recognized the stringency of their accounts of the virtues. Modern liberalism has erred, according to MacIntyre, in giving up this sense of stringency—what Bernard Williams calls the "objective feel" of morality. Since practices involved standards of excellence and obedience to rules (which define the form of activity) as well as the achievement of goods, they "rule out all subjectivist and emotivist analyses of judgment."[6]

Virtues, then, derive from practices: "A virtue is an acquired human quality the possession and exercise of which tends to enable us to achieve those goods which are internal to practices and the lack of which effectively prevents us from achieving any such goods." As cooperative forms of human activity, practices entail relationships between participants that must be characterized by virtues of truthfulness, justice, and courage. While different societies codify these virtues in different ways, MacIntyre maintains that, in one form or another, each and every code "embodies an acknowledgement" of these three virtues.[7]

It should be noted that MacIntyre does not claim that society could not exist without practices and without these virtues. Various technical skills independent of practices and institutions concerned with the pursuit of external goods may perdure without the virtues. However, what MacIntyre regards as the higher expressions of human potential and forms of life cannot exist without practices and the goods that are internal to them. Furthermore, if practices are to survive and flourish, they must be sustained by institutions. MacIntyre illustrates the relationship by saying that "chess, physics, and medicine are practices; chess clubs, laboratories, universities, and hospitals are institutions. . . . [Without the virtues of truthfulness, justice, and courage,] practices could not resist the corrupting power of institutions."[8] Thus, the virtues serve to protect what is most valued in social existence. Where they are absent, the dominant feature of society is competitiveness, as Hobbes's portrait of the state of nature and Turnbull's report of the fate of the Ik make manifest.[9]

The second stage in MacIntyre's account of the concept of virtue involves the identification of "the narrative order of a single human life." As we have observed, MacIntyre believes that "the unity of a human life is the unity of a narrative quest."[10] It is the unity of a life that displays the story of a search for a final *telos*, a "conception of the good for man."[11] The virtues, in addition to sustaining practices,

> also sustain us in the relevant kind of quest for the good, by enabling us to overcome the harms and dangers, temptations and distractions which we encounter, and which will furnish us with increasing self-knowledge and increasing knowledge of the good. . . . The good life for man is the life spent in seeking the good life for man, and the virtues necessary for the seeking are those which enable us to understand what more and what else the good life for man is.[12]

This does not, however, complete MacIntyre's process of development, because everything that has been said so far pertains to persons *qua* individuals. A third stage is necessary to account for our status as social beings.

Since persons find themselves placed in a variety of roles, the story of one's life is embedded in the stories of those communities of which one is a part. Those communities have histories, and their stories are stretched out in time. Thus, each of us is the bearer of a tradition that may weigh heavily or lightly on our shoulders. MacIntyre defines a tradition as "an historically extended, socially embodied argument, and an argument precisely in part about the goods which constitute that tradition."[13]

> Hence the individual's search for his or her good is generally and characteristically conducted within a context defined by those traditions of which the individual's life is a part, and this is true both of those goods which are internal to practices and the goods of a single life. . . . The narrative phenomenon of embedding is crucial. . . . the history of each of our lives is generally and characteristically embedded in and made intelligible in terms of the larger and longer histories of a number of traditions.[14]

With this third stage in place, MacIntyre's account of the virtues and the narrative shape of the moral life is complete. Only when we know the stories of which we are a part can we know what we are to do.

Education into this knowledge begins in childhood:

It is through hearing stories about wicked stepmothers, lost children, good but misguided kings, wolves that suckle twin boys, youngest sons who receive no inheritance but must make their own way in the world, and eldest sons who waste their inheritance on riotous living and go into exile to live with the swine, that children learn or mislearn both what a child and what a parent is, what the cast of characters may be in the drama into which they have been born and what the ways of the world are. Deprive children of stories and you leave them unscripted, anxious stutterers in their actions as in their words. Hence there is no way to give us an understanding of any society, including our own, except through the stock of stories which constitute its initial dramatic resources. Mythology, in its original sense, is at the heart of things. Vico was right and so was Joyce. And so too of course is that moral tradition from heroic society to its medieval heirs according to which the telling of stories has a key part in educating us into the virtues.[15]

What this education generates is not so much a knowledge of a collection of principles for use in making practical inferences, but rather a "kind of capacity for judgment which the agent possesses in knowing how to select among the relevant stack of maxims and how to apply them in particular situations."[16] It is an ability to face with courage and to find one's way through the hazards and tragedies of life by means of the "map" of a living tradition.

What is the prospect for the success of this education into virtue? Is it possible to keep one's bearings and to follow the narratively displayed map in the cultural wasteland of liberal or bureaucratic individualism? Members of marginal social groups who have not drunk deeply from the wells of the dominant culture have an advantage. They never lost sight of virtue in the first place. But what about the rest of us?

As with any other ethic in MacIntyre's analysis, his proposal can flourish only within a certain kind of social and political environment. Contrary to what one might expect, MacIntyre is not altogether pessimistic that such hospitable contexts can be built. "What matters at this stage is the construction of local forms of community within which civility and intellectual and moral life can be sustained through the new dark ages which are already upon us." However, the historical parallel with the decline of the Roman Empire is inexact in that "this time the barbarians are not waiting beyond

the frontiers; they have already been governing us for quite some time."
That is the uniquely modern predicament in which MacIntyre advises us
to wait, "not for a Godot, but for another—doubtless very different—St.
Benedict."[17]

CRITICAL QUESTIONS

So distinctive and provocative a proposal is bound to elicit critical questions.
The present discussion will proceed in three steps. First, I shall consider
two questions that arise in connection with MacIntyre's first and second
stages and argue that the parts of his cumulative case do not fit together as
comfortably as he supposes. Second, I shall revisit the issues identified in
the preceding chapter—freedom, rules, and relativism—to demonstrate
that MacIntyre's recent work incurs some of the same problems as did
its predecessors. Third, I shall note two more general problems that
lead me to conclude that MacIntyre's constructive account is less than
compelling.

Reduced to its simplest, MacIntyre's basic argument is something like
the following. Virtue is fundamental to morality. Virtue is dependent
upon a conception of the human *telos,* some account of the meaning and
purpose of life. These accounts are displayed in and derived from narratives that are historically and culturally diverse.

In these claims there might seem little to which one might object. Yet, as
Williams cautions, there is something peculiar about virtue. While other
persons and their actions are sometimes appraised as virtuous, virtue
ordinarily does not enter into an agent's deliberation about his action.
"The benevolent or kindhearted person does benevolent things, but does
them under other descriptions, such as 'she needs it,' 'it will cheer him up,'
'it will stop the pain'." Meeting needs, bringing cheer, relieving pain, and
countless other things are the sorts of actions benevolent people do. There
is no simple or single way to describe the considerations that the benevolent person entertains. "The road from ethical considerations that weigh
with a virtuous person to the description of the virtue itself," as Williams
warns, "is a tortuous one, and it is both defined and pitted by the impact
of self-consciousness."[18]

To encourage the cultivation of virtue as "a first-personal exercise"
would be to ask us to contemplate not our actions but the way in which
others might evaluate the way we think about our actions. Williams

correctly sees that this "seems a mis-direction of the ethical attention."[19] His purpose is not to remove virtue from our set of ethical concepts but to restrict it from first-person use. Now MacIntyre, in fairness, is not a moralist exhorting us to cultivate self-consciously the virtuous life. But St. Benedict was, and Williams's reservations are noteworthy when MacIntyre calls for new forms of community in order to nurture virtue.

If MacIntyre inclines toward an uncritical appreciation of virtue, there is, surprisingly, another respect in which he doesn't take it far enough. I refer to the fact that he says very little about the notion of character. While recognizing that virtue is specified in relation to some conception of the human *telos*, he does not develop this idea in terms of character. Yet a conception of character seems to be required.

This is particularly evident when one recalls that he thinks the virtues are conflictual. Once the Greek unity of the virtues is abandoned, the need arises for a way to refer to the unity of an individual life. MacIntyre calls it "the narrative order" of a single human life or "the unity of a narrative quest." In common usage, it is called 'character'. MacIntyre does not adequately correlate character with either the idea of virtue or the unity of a single life.[20] The widespread suspicion voiced by Williams that the notion of character "no longer has any, or enough, sense for us" may explain MacIntyre's reticence, but it does not eliminate the need for 'character' in an ethic of virtue.[21]

Doubtless, MacIntyre could accept the caveat about virtue and, less easily though just as surely, elaborate a conception of character. Nevertheless, it would remain an open question whether his various claims concerning virtue, the unity of a single human life (a.k.a. character), and narrative really cohere with one another. At least, it may be said that his account of them fails to establish that they do.

For example, he claims to have identified "a unitary core concept of the virtues" common to a variety of moral traditions. Yet this seems to be at odds with his general historicism, and the cogency of the claim is thereby undermined, not only by his historical analysis, but also by his appeals to narrative. Recall his contention that a conception of the "good for human life" must be expounded in terms of practices, the narrative unity of an individual human life, and a moral tradition. But these are all plural. There are many and different practices, narratives, and traditions. Moreover, the lives of many individuals seem to lack coherence or "narrative unity." Similarly, some traditions encompass a considerable degree of internal diversity. If these, and particularly the narratives of individuals and communities, are so variegated, how can they be said to yield universal virtues and a common conception of the good?

MacIntyre is aware of the problem. At one point he observes that it is often held that "*either* we can admit the existence of rival and contingently incompatible goods which make incompatible claims to our practical allegiance *or* we can believe in some determinate conception of *the* good for man, but... these are mutually exclusive alternatives. No one can consistently hold both these views."[22] Yet this seems to be precisely what MacIntyre is doing in his arguments for a "unified core concept of the virtues" and for a historicist account of all moral concepts.

However, in his judgment, this posing of the alternatives is mistaken. He insists that "there may be better or worse ways for individuals to live through the tragic confrontation of good with good."[23] What is better or worse is said to depend upon the intelligible narrative that unifies the person's life. Knowledge of these better and worse ways of living is, according to MacIntyre, prerequisite for the recognition of "the good life for man." Of course, no one would deny that persons have preferences and make *ad hoc* judgments about ways of life. It also may be the case that these preferences and judgments are influenced by narratives. However, it is far from clear that the possibility of judgments influenced by narratives adds anything to the justification of MacIntyre's contention about "the good life for man."

As I see it, the quest for the good for human life as such and attention to individual and communal narratives pull in opposite directions. One or the other must be sacrificed, or, at least, qualified. If MacIntyre wishes to defend the unity of the virtues and a notion of *the* human *telos* in a classical sense, he should confine himself to the claim about the propae-deutic function of narratives (that they help to teach us what, in principle, we could learn by other means) or perhaps to the (problematic) assertion that all narratives point in the same direction extolling certain virtues. The alternative is to dispense with narrative entirely. On the other hand, MacIntyre could relinquish his claims to universal virtues and the good for human life and use the concept of narrative to explicate the diversity of virtues, modes of moral consciousness, conceptual frameworks, or histori-cal contexts as he might wish. As it stands, MacIntyre inconsistently appeals to narrative to explain both uniformity and pluralism. As a result, both cases are weakened.[24]

Now, let us see, in turn, where MacIntyre's proposal comes down on the issues of freedom, the status of moral rules, and relativism. As we have

seen, MacIntyre holds that our actions are constituent of "enacted dramatic narratives" that give meaning and shape to our lives. He maintains
that we are not only the characters of these stories but also their authors or,
at least, "co-authors." The qualification regarding authorship is MacIntyre's,
and it suggests that he is aware of what is at stake in this claim. To assert
that we are the authors of our stories would entail grand and sweeping
assumptions about self-awareness, freedom, and individual autonomy. To
the extent that the stories are thought to be uniquely our own, issues of
individuality and uniqueness also arise. If all this were the case, the notion
that the narratives of moral traditions and social communities are indispensable for our moral education and highly influential in the shaping of
our individual stories would be undermined.

On the other hand, if it is more nearly correct that we are assigned roles
and inserted into a story that pre-exists our appearance and over which we
have little, if any, authorial control, the place for freedom would be
constricted severely. Stories would seem to impress us into their pre-
determined plots with no deference to our attitudes, plans, or wishes. In
this view, it seems misleading to speak of the composition of stories that
are uniquely our own or even of the "quest for the narrative unity" of our
lives. Furthermore, our capacity for evaluating traditions and choosing
between narratives is diminished. We would be less able or even unable to
gain critical distance from the stories that seek to subject us and to reject
the roles assigned to us.

Here, too, MacIntyre seems to straddle the issue. He admits that one can
rebel against one's identity within a tradition. At the same time, he
maintains (curiously) that this rebellion is simply a way of expressing one's
identity within that tradition. In fact, he contends that a healthy tradition
constitutes an ongoing argument and embodies "continuities of conflict"
that allow for reformation and renewal. Perhaps so, but what if one's
tradition is unhealthy or moribund? In the postscript, he admits that
traditions sometimes "founder," and restless adherents find reasons for
radically reconstituting or "deserting" them.[25] Does his assertion that
rebellion is a form of expression of a tradition really resolve the tension?

If pushed, he would reply that his view does not represent a deprivation
or limitation on the individual's freedom:

> Without those moral particularities to begin from there would
> never be anywhere to begin; but it is in moving forward from such
> particularity that the search for the good, for the universal, consists.

Yet particularity can never be simply left behind or obliterated. The notion of escaping from it into a realm of entirely universal maxims which belong to man as such . . . is an illusion with painful consequences.[26]

But even if it is granted that one cannot leap beyond any and all traditions or narratives to occupy some neutral space, nevertheless, it would seem that one could reject his or her native tradition in favor of another, or enlist a number of traditions to mount a radical critique of one's own. If MacIntyre wishes to insist that one always remains a prisoner of a tradition, even in self-conscious rebellion against it, he must pay the price in terms of a diminution of freedom and autonomy. Perhaps he would admit that his "rebellion is a form of expression" claim overstates the matter. His real view may be congruent with that of Beardsmore, who, as we saw in the last chapter, merely argues that moral revolutionaries retain some connections with other traditions, including the one they seek to overthrow. That is a reasonable position that does not unduly constrain freedom.

In the preceding chapter, I also indicated that MacIntyre is not prepared to dispense with the concept of moral rules altogether. He recognizes that practices and the relationships they entail are subject to violation. When participants cease to be truthful, just, or courageous, practices break down. Furthermore, persons in community, he says, need "to identify certain types of action as the doing or production of harm of such an order that they destroy the bonds of community in such a way as to render the doing or achieving of good impossible."[27]

One might expect this identification process to yield an account of the moral rules. However, MacIntyre neglects to spell out any such account. Instead, he overleaps the realm of the moral rules into the realm of criminal law. Thus, legal offenses such as "the taking of innocent life," "theft," and "perjury" serve to identify kinds of actions regarded "not simply as bad, but intolerable."[28] From the virtues we learn what is honorable and meritorious; from the law we learn what is punishable. The relation between virtues and laws is reciprocal in that, not only does community require law, but the application of laws can never become so routinized that there is no need for judgment and the virtue of justice. A conception of morality that does not include some conception of rules along with the virtues seems incomplete on MacIntyre's own terms.

It also seems to evoke the specter of relativism. I have argued that MacIntyre strains to explain both "the unified core concept of the virtues" and the plurality of concepts of virtue by appealing to narrative. His positing of narrative as the ground of both "the one and the many" is unconvincing. Since narrative is best suited for an account of the diversity of moral views, the question of relativism is unavoidable. Where, exactly, does MacIntyre stand on this issue?

In his "Postscript to the Second Edition," MacIntyre acknowledges that conversation between traditions, each with its own narrative, is possible. This, of course, assumes that they share at least some common features, without which their speech would be mutually unintelligible. While he grants that one of the camps may "appeal to standards which are simply incommensurable," this need not always be the case:

> It will . . . sometimes . . . be possible for adherents of each tradition to understand and to evaluate — by their own standards — the characterizations of their positions advanced by their rivals. And nothing precludes their discovering that these characterizations reveal to them features of their own positions which had hitherto gone unnoticed or considerations, which by their own standards they ought to have entertained, but had not.[29]

If these revelations are many and serious, or if they identify weaknesses to which there appears no evident solution, one may be moved to revise or even to desert one's tradition.

Nothing in this scenario requires that the conversation partners adopt what Williams has called "the mid-air position." Neither party transcends the particularities of her tradition and narrative to attain some tradition-neutral vantage point. Both the critique and the response are couched in terms of the respective traditions. Thus, it might seem that the charge of relativism has not been rebutted.

MacIntyre admits that relativism has not been defeated, in the sense that the prospect of rationally insuperable disagreement has not been eliminated completely: "My position entails that there are no successful a priori arguments which will guarantee in advance that such a situation could not occur. Indeed nothing could provide us with such a guarantee which did not involve the successful resuscitation of the Kantian transcendental project."[30] Although not defeated, relativism is defused and rendered innocuous.

MacIntyre's position is reminiscent of that of Phillips and Mounce. Once the possibility of a transcendental vantage point is given up, the relativistic implications of 'practices', 'traditions', and 'narratives' are acceptable. We remain free to converse with others, make judgments about and disagree with their traditions, and revise or abandon our own. This is all the freedom we need and, in MacIntyre's view, all to which we are entitled.

Finally, I shall note two more general criticisms of MacIntyre's vision of ethics: that he romanticizes the distant past and that he violates his historicism when he commends an Aristotelianism *nouveau*. Many critics detect in his critique of modernity, with its exquisite sensitivity to the perils of the present, a highly uncritical appreciation for life in the storied past.[31] As one reviewer observes, "after virtue is after Eden, but it is also after hierarchy, after slavery, after superstition and after ignorance."[32] To concur with this judgment one need not overlook the fact that we live also after Auschwitz and on the brink of nuclear Armageddon. All that one might ask of MacIntyre is a more dialectical and nuanced assessment of both the past and the present.

More important than quibbles about the tone of MacIntyre's historical narrative, however, is the question of the adequacy of his counsel for the present and future. Is it not uncharacteristically ahistorical of MacIntyre to attempt to "vindicate" Aristotle's ethics? Even if the metaphysical biology and other anachronisms could be left behind, would not the remodeled Aristotelianism be just another "fragment"? The reviewer quoted above finds in MacIntyre's proposal an "antihistorical intellectualism" that is "preposterous" on the evidence of his own analysis: "The crux of his argument is precisely that it is not so much virtue as the social structures and cultural ethos from which it grew that have been 'irrevocably lost.' If this is so, vindicating Aristotle is an exercise in despair."[33] To these criticisms, MacIntyre acknowledges that "an historicist defense of Aristotle is bound to strike some skeptical critics as a paradoxical as well as a Quixotic enterprise" and places it on the agenda for a future volume.

When introducing this section, I indicated that on the basis of these critical questions I do not find MacIntyre's proposal compelling. Of course, the status he claims for his view is not one "necessarily to be assented to by any rational being because invulnerable or almost invulnerable to objections." Instead of "a perfect theory," he offers us what *may* be "the best theory so far."[34]

His criteria for establishing that a theory is "the best so far" are three. It must have: (1) "successfully transcended the limitations of its predecessors and in so doing provided the best means available for understanding those predecessors to date"; (2) "confronted successive challenges from a number of rival points of view but in each case have been able to modify itself in the ways required to incorporate the strengths of those points of view while avoiding their weaknesses and limitations"; and (3) "provided the best explanation so far of those weaknesses and limitations."[35] MacIntyre does not assert that he has "as yet sustained the claim" that his ethic of virtue shaped by narrative meets the criteria and is, thus, "the best theory so far."[36] To be sure, he is, nonetheless, confident that the superiority of his theory can be demonstrated.

For reasons that should be clear by now, I do not share his confidence. Assuming that the internal incoherencies I identified could be removed and the Aristotelianism updated, there would still be the matter of MacIntyre's neglect of the moral rules. The Kantian project may not be as moribund as MacIntyre supposes. Moreover, updating Aristotle by jettisoning certain antique views of man, nature, and community is, in itself, not a simple thing. As Williams says, "no one has yet found a good way of doing without those assumptions," something that MacIntyre needs to do if the gap created by the loss of *the* human *telos* is to be closed.[37]

5

USES OF NARRATIVE
IN CONTEMPORARY THEOLOGY

Narratives, as we have seen in the preceding chapters, play an important role in shaping our understanding of ourselves, our communities, our histories, and our morality. Among contemporary American Christian theologians, the significance of narrative for theological methodology is widely heralded. Just as in the philosophical literature, narrative, or story, is understood here in different ways and employed to different ends. This chapter identifies some of these proposals regarding the theological function of narrative and analyzes them as belonging to either a liberal-universalistic or a postliberal-particularistic tradition. If stories influence morality in general, and if story is crucial to the religious self-understanding of the Christian community, then one would expect narrative to be vital to the work of Christian ethics. By examining the second premise, this chapter lays the groundwork for the next two chapters, in which I shall explore the implications for theological ethics.

COMMON FEATURES

Despite the diversity, it has been suggested that there is a "shared central contention among those who claim a necessary relationship between theology and narrative" to the effect that "the religious convictions which are at the heart of theological reflection depend on narrative for their intelligibility and significance."[1]

> The primary claim of a "narrative theologian" is that in order justifiably to elucidate, examine and transform those deeply held religious beliefs that make a community what it is, one must necessarily show regard for and give heed to those linguistic structures which, through their portrayal of the contingent interaction between persons and events, constitute the source and ground of such beliefs. In short, the fundamental contention is that an adequate theology must attend to narrative.[2]

However, as we shall see, the stories to which narrative theologians attend are as different as the theologies narrativists generate.

Also, it has been observed that many narrative theologians share a common indebtedness to the thought of H. Richard Niebuhr, specifically, to his use of 'story' in explicating the meaning of revelation.[3] Niebuhr insisted that "we are in history as the fish is in water and what we mean by the revelation of God can be indicated only as we point through the medium in which we live."[4] In order to "point" through history, Niebuhr found it necessary to distinguish between "external" and "internal" history.

External history objectifies the succession of past events and records them in an impersonal and disinterested manner. Internal history, on the other hand, apprehends past events "from within, as items in the destiny of persons and communities," and interprets them "in a context of persons with their resolutions and devotions." Internal history is deeply personal but not solipsistic, because it is mediated through "a community of selves." Within this community, selves are internally related and members of each other. To become a member of a community of selves is to "adopt its past as our own" and thereby to be "changed in our present existence." Internal history "can be communicated and persons can refresh as well as criticize each other's memories of what has happened to them in the common life; on the basis of a common past they can think together about the common future."[5] Thus, to speak of revelation in the Christian church is to refer to the history of selves within the community and to history as it is lived and apprehended from within.

This referring is confessional, and it takes the form of a story. The New Testament shows how the earliest Christians confessed their faith by telling the story of their life: "Their story was not a parable which could be replaced by another; it was irreplaceable and untranslatable. An internal compulsion rather than free choice led them to speak of what they knew by telling about Jesus Christ and their relation to God through him." According to Niebuhr, Christians of every time and place have the same need. The church as a living community is always compelled "to say truly what it stands for," and is unable "to do so otherwise than by telling the story of its life."[6] Since these remarks were more suggestive than fully explained, it is not surprising that subsequent theologians influenced by Niebuhr's use of story have developed his suggestion in a variety of ways.

SOME CLASSIFICATORY DISTINCTIONS

Before sketching several of these developments, I wish to introduce some distinctions between various ways of understanding religion and theology. These distinctions will help to elucidate the difference between the disparate theological uses of narrative.

I shall be applying what George Lindbeck identifies as three theories or models for understanding and studying a religion.[7] Since his models have generated considerable controversy, I should state that I take Lindbeck's models to be "ideal types." It can remain an open question whether individual theologians (especially major theologians whose thought is rich, subtle, and complex) conform completely to a type. Nevertheless, insofar as typologies identify and illumine certain themes or tendencies, they can be heuristically useful.

The first of Lindbeck's models for understanding a religion is designated as the "cognitivist" because it views religions as collections of true or false propositions. It is sometimes held to be the model that is most descriptive of the Christian tradition, although questions may be raised as to whether certain notable figures within the tradition (for example, Luther or Aquinas) would recognize it as an adequate characterization. Nevertheless, it is hospitable to truth claims, albeit at the expense of offering potential for interreligious dialogue. Its fatal flaw, however, lies in its negligible survival value in a post-Kantian intellectual climate.

The second approach is the "experiential-expressive" model, which understands a religion to be a system of "non-informative and non-discursive symbols" that objectify and evoke fundamental "inner feelings, attitudes or existential orientations."[8] When it is accompanied by the view that these attitudes are universal, the experiential-expressive model seems well suited for the study of comparative religion and for interreligious dialogue of the "We're all really saying the same thing only in different ways" variety. As Lindbeck correctly observes, there is much in the contemporary *Zeitgeist* that conduces toward the embracing of this model. But however one may assess its popularity, the experiential-expressive model has its limitations. While it is easy enough to maintain that the symbols generated under the model are related in some way to that which is (or, in a weaker sense, is taken to be) transcendent, it is very difficult to sustain any truth claims about particular symbols or symbol systems against the tides of historicism and cultural relativism.

Paul Tillich's extensive reflection on religious symbols serves as a case in point. While granting that the symbolizations of many religions were subjectively true, Tillich maintained that only Christian symbols (specifically, the cross of Christ) were "non-idolatrously" and objectively related to the truly Ultimate. According to Tillich, Christian symbols were superior because they were derived from the level of the human person; the man Jesus pointed beyond himself, and the symbol of his cross was 'self-negating'. However, none of these claims is uniquely Christian. For example, the Jataka tradition of Mahayana Buddhism in which Buddhas give themselves to be eaten by wild beasts could be said to be as self-negating as John 12:44 or the cross of Christ. Although Tillich never formally withdrew his claim for Christianity's objective superiority, in his last years he apparently could find no grounds for asserting it as he sought to "encounter" the world's religions. The experiential-expressive model, even in the hands of a thinker of Tillich's genius, cannot adequately handle the truth claims of Christian doctrines, unless it were simply to posit their truth value in a realm where anthropology and sociology do not corrupt nor psychologists break in and steal. However, this move would compromise the model's utility in dialogue.

The third way of understanding a religion is to view it as a cultural-linguistic system. A religion can be seen as "a kind of cultural and/or linguistic framework or medium that shapes the entirety of life and thought . . . [as an] idiom that makes possible the description of realities, the formulation of beliefs, and the experiencing of inner attitudes, feelings and sentiments."[9] As communal phenomena, the stories, symbols, and rituals constitute and shape the subjectivities of individuals. They are not simply manifestations of those subjectivities, as they are under the experiential-expressive model. In this way, a religion, like a Wittgensteinian "language game," is correlated with a form of life that has both cognitive and behavioral dimensions.

Lindbeck's three models for the study of religion may be correlated with two different modes of theology distinguished by Hans Frei. The cognitive and experiential-expressive models are most naturally related to a conception of theology as religions-encompassing. In this view, theology is a foundational enterprise of which specifically Christian theology is a subset. Here, theology is "discourse about a concept, 'God', and the usual assumption has been that part of what the inquiry is about is whether or not or how the concept 'refers'." Theological discourse is essentially philosophical in that philosophy is "the 'foundation' discipline providing all-fields-encompassing arguments and criteria for meaning and certainty, in the light of which it arbitrates what may count as meaningful language, genuine thought and knowledge."[10] Of course, the philosophy may vary materially (it may be analytic, phenomenological, structuralist, etc.), but some overarching philosophical scheme is required.

Theology in the second mode is religion-specific:

> 'Theology' here is an aspect of the self-description of Christianity [as a specific religion among others], rather than *Christian* theology being one instance of 'theology' as a general class. It is an inquiry into the coherence and appropriateness of any given instance of the use of Christian language in the light of its normative articulation, whether that be scripture, tradition, the Christian conscience, a mixture of these and other candidates.[11]

This view of theology is correlative to the cultural-linguistic model of religion. "It is a second-order discipline dependent on the first-order language of the religion."[12]

Since the language in question is the language of a community, "a social organism," theology is "closer to the social sciences [sociology of religion, cultural anthropology, etc.] than to philosophy, though certainly not identical with them." The community of adherents, its elite, its set of rituals, beliefs, and attitudes, the narratives of its sacred text along with its interpretive tradition and the relations between all of the above are "not the *signs* or *manifestations* of the religion; they *constitute* it, in complex and changing coherence." Both the social scientist and the theologian focus (albeit in different ways) on the 'stuff' of the religion, the latter operating as an adherent or agent of its self-description. Christian theology in this second mode is "normed description of the Christian religion and of its language as a social phenomenon."[13]

Earlier I noted that the experiential-expressive model does not make adequate provision for the finality of Christian truth claims as uniquely and unsurpassably true. What sort of meaning could the cultural-linguistic model (and the kind of theology correlated with it) assign to the notion of unsurpassable truth? In the cognitive model, unsurpassable truth means propositional truth based on ontological correspondence. If one religion's propositions actually correspond to the way things are, discrepant propositions of other religions are false. Truth under the experiential-expressive model refers to the degree to which a symbol has evocative power. But in the cultural-linguistic model, truth is, first of all, intrasystemic or contextual. The focus is on the religion's categories and their adequacy: "Adequate categories are those which can be made to apply to what is taken to be real, and which therefore make possible, though they do not guarantee, propositional, practical and symbolic truth. A religion which is thought of as having such categories can be said to be 'categorially true.' "[14] Truth in the cultural-linguistic model is the capacity for truthful communication.

According to Lindbeck, the "categorial" truth of the cultural-linguistic model is stronger than the "symbolic" truth of the experiential-expressive model.[15] Since there can be no logically intrinsic upper limit on the evocative power of symbols, it is impossible for the experiential-expressive model to assign much meaning to the notion of "unsurpassable truth." Categorial truth is stronger than symbolic truth because it allows that there may be only one religion whose concepts and categories actually refer to what is, in fact, more important than anything else in the universe. In that event, other religions would be categorially false and religiously meaningless because their categories would fail to comprise the necessary conditions for the possibility of either propositional or expressive truth or falsity. At the same time, categorial truth is weaker than propositional truth because the possibility of false affirmations is not excluded in *a priori* fashion. Nevertheless, Lindbeck observes that a religion understood as a cultural-linguistic system correlated with a worldview and form of life may (though it need not) be pictured as "a single gigantic proposition" that may or may not correspond ontologically to the way things are. The model also allows one to confess fideistically the objective truth of the individual propositions or to attempt their defense by a variety of means, including transcendental deductions, process metaphysics, or cumulative arguments other than those of proof or strict probability.[16] In any case, the cultural-linguistic model can assign a strong intrasystemic meaning and allow for the strongest ontological meaning for the notion of unsurpassable truth.

Ironically, alleged experiential-expressivists have joined cognitivists in charging that it is Lindbeck's favored cultural-linguistic model that is soft on truth.[17] While I cannot join the debate here, some of the criticisms are misplaced. A questionable capacity for ontological truth claims seems more problematic for narrative or postliberal theologies developed within the cultural-linguistic model than it does for the cultural-linguistic model itself. After all, the cultural-linguistic model *per se* is intended to offer a neutral account of what a religion is. The question of truth concerns the adequacy of the religion's categories. The primacy of "categorial truth" in no way excludes the possibility of ontological truth. But neither does the cultural-linguistic model simply assume that the religion's claims are ontologically true. Is this a weakness in such a model? Would a model that stipulated the ontological truth of a religion be of any use to non-theological students of religion? The answer to both questions is no. Normative theological appropriations of the cultural-linguistic model would need to adopt one of the strategies mentioned above or some other to defend their truth claims. The relative adequacy of these means of defense is an important issue for theologians and philosophers of religion to pursue. But its unsettled status detracts neither from the model itself nor from my use of it.

With Lindbeck's models of religion and Frei's modes of theology in mind, now let us see how a number of theologians are using the category of narrative.

EXPERIENTIAL-EXPRESSIVE USES

Many of the theologians writing about story today are committed to an anthropological thesis that holds narrative to be the universal inner form of human experience. Personal identity and self-understanding are held to depend upon our capacity to understand, even if only implicitly, our experience through time as a single, continuous story. An influential version of this thesis concerning the narrative quality of experience has been stated by Stephen Crites. Describing the phenomenon of memory and anticipation, Crites says:

> The inner form of any possible experience is determined by the union of these three modalities [past, present, and future] in every

moment of experience.... The tensed unity of these modalities requires narrative forms both for its expression (mundane stories) and for its own sense of the meaning of its internal coherence (sacred stories). For this tensed quality is already an incipient narrative form.[18]

In addition to our individual stories, we also require what Crites calls "sacred" stories. "These are stories that orient the life of people through time, their life-time, their individual and corporate existence and their sense of style, to the great powers that establish the reality of their world." Sacred stories are not anyone's self-conscious creation. Rather, they are culturally given, and it is the sacred story itself that "creates a world of consciousness and the self that is oriented to it."[19] Thus, Crites maintains that sacred stories hold a kind of normative authority over our mundane, individual stories and set the stage for our being in the world.

Versions of the anthropological thesis about personal stories and the additional claim concerning sacred stories underlie a host of recent theological applications of narrative. Of course, narrative can mean several things and be used in a variety of ways. Three types of use are described below.[20]

First, narrative, or story, can be employed to explicate the phenomenon of religion in human experience.[21] Here, as George Stroup observes,

> "narrative" is used to describe and explain the location of religion in human experience and the meaning of "faith" in relation to a person's encounter with other people and the world. The "religious dimension" of human experience is interpreted as having something to do with the narratives people recite about themselves or the narratives they use in order to structure and make sense out of the world. An ambiguity that often emerges in these discussions is whether narrative is the form through which one gets at that reality which is the source of religion in human experience, or whether narrative . . . is itself the bearer of the sacred.[22]

Vagueness pervades much of this literature. Little, if any, attempt is made to explain what precisely is meant by story or to distinguish between autobiography, novels, poems, scripture, fables, myths, and so forth. Michael Goldberg, Stroup, and other critics have noted that the various narrative forms may be related to historical claims and to truth in different ways; yet the narratives, by and large, ignore these differences and the issues behind them. Of course, by taking narratives of all sorts to be various expressions of some fact about universal human experience, the narrativists seem to presuppose the "experiential-expressive" model of religion. Thus, it is not surprising that they do not make strong truth claims for particular narratives.

Second, narrative can be used as a heuristic category for introducing Christian theology and truth claims. Often it is used in a very general way to refer to the basic substance of the Christian faith. For example, Robert Jenson's *Story and Promise* briefly summarizes the Christian "story" as:

> "There has lived a man wholly for others, all the way to death; and he has risen, so that his self-giving will finally triumph." . . . Christianity is the lived-out fact of the telling and mistelling, believing and perverting, practice and malpractice, of the narrative of what is supposed to have happened and to be yet going to happen with Jesus-in-Israel, and of the promise made by that narrative.[23]

Jenson provides a miniature systematic theology spelling out the "message" of the church. In his execution of this task there is little further reference to story. While this lacuna in no way detracts from the quality of his dogmatics, it suggests that, for him, the category 'narrative' does little work and is inessential. His purposes could be served without appeal to story.

The same is true of Gabriel Fackre's *Christian Story: A Narrative Interpretation of Basic Christian Doctrine*. Stroup maintains that it is "unclear whether 'story' refers to a set of narratives in Scripture, a set of doctrines, the experience of Christian individuals or communities, or a combination of some or all of these."[24] While Fackre introduces the various doctrines as "the chapter headings of the Christian story," they are not narrative in form, leading Stroup to doubt that 'story' *per se* is of any particular significance for Fackre's overall project.

A somewhat more fully developed dogmatic use of story is David Harned's exploration of the meaning of the Apostles' Creed and its function within the church. Harned states that "the Creed shares with the New Testament a form which is essentially narrative. Christianity is not first of all a world view but a story. . . . " The Creed provides what Harned calls "a master image," the image of the self as a "child of God," which motivates the believer to develop a coherent, consistent character in accordance with the narrative. Harned is clearly committed to the thesis concerning the narrative quality of human experience. "We need stories that convey a sense of an ending which can invest our past and present with the meaning and coherence" they would otherwise lack. The creedal summary of the biblical narrative, when confessed, becomes an avowal of Christian identity. Through the work of the Holy Spirit in the Christian community, the story of God's acts "*becomes* God's story for us, as well as our own story."[25] In Harned's hands, narrative is put to work to a far greater extent than it is in the hands of Jenson or Fackre.

The third use of narrative in recent theological literature focuses on personal life-stories and the way in which they display convictions. A few theologians have published autobiographical essays, while the more reserved have confined themselves to discussions of the role of autobiography in theology.[26] Others have taken a renewed interest in the biographies of exemplary personages. James McClendon, for example, believes that (somehow) contemporary theology will be "remade" if only theologians attend to the life-stories of persons like Dag Hammarskjöld, Martin Luther King, Jr., Clarence Jordan, and Charles Ives.[27] Yet even sympathetic commentators such as Stroup and Goldberg (who has given these works careful attention) warn that the emphasis on life-stories raises serious literary and philosophical issues that are largely unexamined in the literature. Precisely how is one to interpret the "text" of a life, one's own or someone else's? How are rationalization and falsification by means of an artificial coherence to be avoided? In autobiography, the danger of self-deception is acute.[28] A less sympathetic critic, Ted Estess, decries "the tendency [in this literature] of viewing story as the only 'motion of consciousness' [and the implication that] story is by itself an adequate metaphor for interpreting human experience."[29] Each of these caveats is, in my judgment, well founded. As Stroup himself recognizes, it is defects such as these that fuel "the widespread suspicion that 'story' is only another theological fad, another admission by contemporary theology that it has nothing of significance to say, that theologians cannot 'do' theology but can only talk about themselves."[30]

To summarize, all of the theological uses of story sketched above subscribe to the general anthropological thesis regarding the narrative quality of human experience. Thus, they assume the experiential-expressive model of religion. They are committed to the claims that there is such a thing as universal experience and that it has a narrative quality or shape. Both claims are highly controvertible. There is a sense in which these proponents of story are doing theology in what Frei describes as the foundational mode, though they are hardly self-conscious regarding many of those foundational philosophical issues. In fact, their avoidance of philosophical issues concerning meaning and truth undermines the plausibility of their proposals. If you have your story and I have mine, is it possible to say which, if either, is more nearly true? Would it be the one that is more evocative of universal human experience? How could that be determined? Could it be said that one story is "unsurpassably" true? What would it mean for a personal life-story to be true? What is the normative relation between my story and "the Christian story"? Where are the lines of authority? These questions point to some of the problems attendant to story theologies of this sort.

CULTURAL-LINGUISTIC USES

Far more promising are those theological uses of narrative that are agnostic with respect to the general anthropological thesis and adhere to the theological method appropriate to the cultural-linguistic model of religion. These uses focus on biblical narrative and its function within the Christian community. What is true there may or may not be generalizable with respect to other narratives and communities.

In his influential work on the hermeneutics of biblical narrative, Hans Frei observes that interpretation of scripture underwent a sea change in the eighteenth century with the advent of historical criticism. Prior to that time,

> Western Christian reading of the Bible ... was usually strongly realistic, i.e., at once literal and historical, and not only doctrinal or edifying. The words and sentences meant what they said, and because they did so they accurately described real events and real truths that were rightly put only in those terms and no others. Other ways of reading portions of the Bible, for example, in a spiritual or allegorical sense, were permissible, but they must not offend against a literal reading of those parts which seemed most obviously to demand it. Most eminent among them were all those stories which together went into the making of a single storied or historical sequence. ... Christian preachers and theological commentators ... envisioned the real world as formed by the sequence told by the biblical stories.[31]

Despite a resurgence of this way of reading in the Renaissance and the Reformation, in the eighteenth century it began to disappear.

Precritical literal or realistic readings assumed that the biblical stories described "actual historical occurrences" and that "the real historical world" thus described was "a single world of one temporal sequence." In order to understand scripture as a unified cumulative story, or narrative, depicting that world, the literal reader regarded "earlier biblical stories as figures or types of later stories and of their events and patterns of meaning." This figural or typological reading was "at once a literary and historical procedure" that rendered a common narrative and a single history. Moreover, the realistic reader recognized "a duty to fit himself into that world in which he was in any case a member" and to do so "in part by figural interpretation and in part of course by his mode of life." The basic interpretive direction was from the biblical narrative to the contemporary world, "incorporating extra-biblical thought, experience and reality into the one real world detailed and made accessible by the biblical story—not the reverse."[32]

Frei's careful study of eighteenth- and nineteenth-century hermeneutics explains how this way of reading scripture was eclipsed by modern methods that reversed the interpretive direction. Meaning and truth came to be seen as separate questions. As historical awareness called the historical accuracy of biblical stories into question, it was necessary to detach the meaning of the story from the words themselves literally understood. Questions regarding meaning and truth were answerable only from outside the story itself. "Figural interpretation became discredited both as a literary device and as a historical argument" and "faded into oblivion as a means for relating the world of biblical narrative to present experience and to the world of extra-biblical events, experiences and concepts."[33] Historical criticism and biblical theology, the successors of the literal and figural readings of biblical narrative, came to be seen as very different enterprises, and their relation became problematic. One aspect of this problem, the relation between scripture and ethics, will be discussed in the following chapter.

Fortunately, in Frei's opinion, realistic reading of biblical narrative is neither extinct nor confined to intellectual backwaters of fundamentalism. Karl Barth's biblical exegesis exemplifies the kind of narrative reading that Frei believes can still be done in the wake of the developments he describes. Barth "distinguishes historical from realistic reading of the theologically most significant biblical narratives without falling into the trap of instantly

making history the test of the *meaning* of the realistic form of the stories."[34]
Barth recognizes that, in realistic narrative, form and meaning are inextricably linked. The meaning of the story is a function of the interaction between character and circumstance. There is no need to infer or abstract anything (such as a mode of consciousness or a way of being in the world) from the story that might then be translated into some putatively more accessible idiom. The stories literally mean what they say.

David Kelsey observes that Barth often construed biblical narratives as "identity descriptions" displayed in characteristic patterns of intention and action. These patterns render a character, God, and serve to authorize Barth's theological proposals.

> It is as though Barth took scripture to be one vast, loosely structured non-fictional novel—at least Barth takes it to be non-fiction! The characteristic patterns in the narrative guide what the theologian says about the agent/subject of the stories, in much the way that patterns in a novel guide what a literary critic may say about the characters in a novel.[35]

The principal character in the Bible (God throughout and Jesus in the New Testament) is described in a way that is irreducibly particular to the world of biblical narrative. No other stories and no other world can yield the same description.

According to Frei, Barth's entire theological project was a "conceptual description" or "redescription of the temporal world of eternal grace." His purpose was to show:

> (1) that this world [the world of biblical narrative] is a world with its own linguistic integrity, much as a literary art work is a consistent work in its own right, one that we can have only under a depiction, under its own particular depiction and not any other, and certainly not in pre-linguistic immediacy or in experience without depiction; but (2) that unlike any other depicted world it is the one common world in which we all live and move and have our being. To indicate all this he will use scriptural exegesis to illustrate his themes; he will do ethics to indicate that this narrated, narratable world is at the same time the ordinary world in which we are responsible for our actions; and he will do *ad hoc* apologetics, in order to throw into relief particular features of this world by

distancing them from or approximating them to other descriptions of the same or other linguistic worlds.[36]

It is important to realize that "instead of re-describing the contents of the Christian sources in terms of a new language and situation," as do most modern theologians, in Barth's program "it is the contemporary language and situation which are redescribed and incorporated into the world of biblical narrative."[37]

Besides identifying the distinctive features of biblical narrative, describing their eclipse in the Enlightenment and their recovery in the work of Karl Barth, Frei provides a constructive account of what a realistic narrative reading of the Gospels might look like. In *The Identity of Jesus Christ: The Hermeneutical Bases of Dogmatic Theology*, Frei suggests that the Gospel narrative may be regarded as a story that sets forth the individual, specific, and unsubstitutable identity of Jesus. The narrative renders Jesus as an agent with characteristic behaviors, attributes, and dispositions. His identity is disclosed "in the mysterious coincidence of his intentional action with circumstances partly initiated by him, partly devolving upon him."[38] As the reader sees how Jesus' intentions are enacted in the story, he or she comes to know who Jesus is. Moreover, and specifically in his resurrection,

> he is the man from Nazareth who redeemed men by his helplessness, in perfect obedience enacting their good in their behalf. As that same one, he was raised from the dead and manifested to be their redeemer. As that same one, Jesus the redeemer, he cannot *not* live, and to conceive of him as not living is to misunderstand who he is. To know who he is to believe in his self-focused presence. This, it appears, is the testimony of the New Testament and, hence, the understanding of believers. His identity and his presence are given together in indissoluble unity.[39]

Attempts to seek the presence of Christ otherwise, say in our religious self-consciousness, fail to appreciate the meaning of the Gospel story and, more often than not, end in frustration.

On the basis of these works, Goldberg reckons Frei to be one of a "new breed of narrative theologians." Frei would not be pleased with this appellation, in part because, as Goldberg fails to recognize, his use of narrative is very different from that of the other theologians so classified.

Frei clearly distinguishes himself from those theologians who assume the experiential-expressive model of religion and a foundational theological method:

> I am not proposing or arguing a general anthropology. I am precisely *not* claiming that narrative sequence is the built-in constitution of human being phenomenologically uncovered. That may or may not be the case. Rather, I am suggesting that it is narrative specificity through which we describe an intentional-agential world and ourselves in it. If there *is* a "narrative theology", the meaning of that term in the context of the self-description of the Christian community is that we are specified by relation to its particular narrative and by our conceptual redescription of it in belief and life, not by a quality of "narrativity" inherent in our picture of self and world at large.[40]

If Frei's work is to be understood correctly, it must be viewed in the context of a cultural-linguistic model of religion, with theology being the self-description of the Christian community and its first-order religious language. Those critics who wait upon Frei to provide a general anthropology and hermeneutics are not likely to be satisfied.

I do not mean to suggest, however, that interest in a general hermeneutics necessarily commits one to the experiential-expressive model of religion. Paul Ricoeur, to whom Frei's critics often look for a comprehensive theory of textual interpretation, should not be classified among the experiential-expressivists I have mentioned. His interest in narrative antedates and enriches, while it manifestly transcends, the current concern for "narrative theology." For Ricoeur, the relationship between experience and language is complex and dialectical. His work toward a universal hermeneutics of the language of symbol, metaphor, and communal myth is intended, ultimately, to disclose the full meaning and reference of particular texts (e.g., biblical narratives).[41]

Ricoeur and those who share his vision worry that Frei may be trapped within the deconstructionist labyrinth of intratextuality.[42] By concentrating on the meaning of biblical texts and by bringing their reference into close proximity, if not into identification, with their meaning, Frei neglects to show how biblical narratives are true. This is, in Ricoeur's eyes, a serious omission that cripples the theological enterprise. His own hermeneutical investigations aspire to demonstrate the way in which narratives speak truthfully about temporality and human experience.

Specifically, Goldberg and others charge that Frei's observation that biblical narrative is "history-like" in character seems indifferent to historical facticity. Goldberg believes that for stories such as these, which are used to warrant various theological claims, "the question of 'whether it really happened' cannot be ignored without theological peril."[43] He judges Frei's answer to be "ambiguous" and, therefore, his theological proposals to "stand unjustified no matter what might be their merits on the . . . affective 'transformational' plane."[44] This judgment cannot be sustained. Frei is simply calling attention to the history-like quality of realistic narrative. Certainly, he does not try to argue that this quality is evidence of historical facticity, but the claim that the stories actually do refer to historical occurrences is in no way precluded. 'History-likeness' (literal meaning) and history (ostensive reference) ought not to be confused or conflated. It is precisely "the hermeneutical reduction of the former to an aspect of the latter" that put biblical narrative into eclipse.[45] That Frei refuses, in his constructive work, "to speak speculatively or evidentially" about such matters as the resurrection of Christ, "while nevertheless affirming it as an indispensable Christian claim," does not render his position "ambiguous."[46] In fact, he is quite explicit, as, for example, when he says:

> I shall not attempt to evaluate the *historical* reliability of the Gospel story of Jesus or argue the unique truth of the story on grounds of a true, factual "kernel" in it. Instead, I shall be focusing on its character as a story. As for history, I shall take for granted . . . what most commentators agree upon: that a man, Jesus of Nazareth, who proclaimed the Kingdom of God's nearness, did exist and was finally executed.[47]

One may wish that such historical claims were demonstrated or defended and not simply taken for granted, but they are not, for all of that, ambiguous. While Frei's theology of Christian self-description within a cultural-linguistic model of religion speaks, first of all, on the level of "categorial" truth, it does allow for the possibility of positing and defending propositional truth claims and is in no way hostile toward attempts to do so.

"NARRATIVE THEOLOGY"

As I have indicated, Frei's treatment of biblical narrative is quite specific and fairly modest. He certainly does not attempt to provide anything like a full-blown narrative theology. A more ambitious and self-consciously narrative theological program — the most fully developed to date — is that of Stroup's *Promise of Narrative Theology*. Stroup fears that, in most of the theological proposals on behalf of story, narrative is little more than a "propaedeutic" to doctrinal theology proper — a bridge between first-order religious language and theology's second-order critical reflection. Thinking this to be inadequate, Stroup argues that narrative is "indispensable": "Narrative is an important theological category because it is essential for understanding human identity and what happens to the identity of persons in that process Christians describe by means of the doctrine of revelation."[48]

Stroup uses 'narrative' in a twofold sense: as a description of a literary genre and as "a hermeneutical process or mode of understanding that takes place in Christian faith." From these uses Stroup derives a category he calls "Christian narrative," which is similar to a form of religious autobiography or confession, as classically exemplified by Augustine. Christian narrative "emerges from the interaction or collision between the identity narratives of individuals and the identity narratives of the Christian community." More concerned with the hermeneutical process than the literary genre, Stroup says that "to understand Christian narrative properly is to be able to reinterpret one's personal identity by means of the biblical texts, history of tradition, and theological doctrines which make up the church's narrative." When one's self-understanding is reinterpreted in this way, "revelation becomes a reality in the subjective experience of individuals and communities."[49]

It is unclear whether Stroup subscribes to the experiential-expressive or the cultural-linguistic model of religion and their cognate theological methods. Actually, he seems to ally himself to both. On the one hand, he assumes that narrative has "an almost primordial location in human experience" and stipulates that "every philosophical anthropology . . . which claims to offer a full description of human being must come to terms with the narrative structure of human identity." On the other hand, he thinks that Wittgenstein's analysis of language and forms of life illumines "many of the dynamics . . . at the center of [his] description of life in the Christian community and the nature of Christian identity."[50] These two commitments pull Stroup in opposite directions. One wonders whether narrative or revelation (that which Christian confession may become) is, for Stroup, the controlling term. Given his concern for the loss of Christian identity, both personal and communal, and "biblical illiteracy" in the church, I suspect that he is more closely wedded to the cultural-linguistic model. For the sake of consistency (and perhaps plausibility as well), he ought to remain agnostic with respect to the narrative quality of human experience.

Of course, if something analogous to Crites's thesis is withdrawn, there may be less reason for Stroup to insist that narrative is an indispensable category for systematic theology. Still, it might be imagined to have an apologetic utility in light of certain contemporary philosophical discussions of epistemology.[51] But this would not seem to be Stroup's fundamental reason for retaining the claim about the centrality of narrative. His basic attachment is to identity and narrative's role in expressing it. Some of his statements about identity are so sweeping as to suggest that every Christian must (or, at least, ought to) compose a spiritual autobiography. At the risk of overstating Stroup's intention, I submit that there is a kind of narcissistic preciousness to the idea that we are the artificers of our own identities in the sense of self-consciously creating an artifact. In any case, Stroup is manifestly sanguine about the prospects for self-awareness and sanctification.

For example, he says that "the individual's decision to see and live in the world by means of [the narrative of the Christian community] is what Christians call 'faith' and the process by which the community's faith and narrative become the individual's is what Christians refer to as 'conversion'." This description of 'faith' as a "*decision* to see and live" in certain ways differs radically from other Christian conceptions of 'faith' that refer to basic trust in divine mercy, made possible not by resolution but by grace. While Stroup does describe this encounter between the individual and the Christian narrative as a "collision" rather than a smooth appropriation, nonetheless, it seems too effortless and easy. At the same time, it must be said that Stroup, unlike many of the other proponents of story, is clear regarding the lines of authority: "To live in the Christian community is to share a commitment that its traditions and its narratives are more appropriate than those of other communities and other traditions for making decisions and interpreting the world."[52] With Barth, Stroup moves from the Christian sources to the world.

Stroup's account of Christian self-identity has noteworthy implications for theological ethics. Describing the function of narrative in Israel's faith and life as illustrated in Deuteronomy, Stroup discovers that

> there is a dialectical relationship between the narrative of redemption history and the testimonies, statutes and ordinances which govern Israel's life. On the one hand, the Deuteronomists believe that Israel's narrative history is the context for understanding and obeying the law. . . . On the other hand . . . the narrative cannot be recited casually or disinterestedly. It is a narrative that demands to be embodied and lived and Israel's statutes provide the context for the enactment of the narrative.[53]

The observation that in the Bible laws are thought to be fully intelligible only within the narrative context is an important one. Attention to narrative may contribute to an eventual resolution of the long-standing and notorious problem of how scripture and ethics are to be related. According to Stroup:

> In the hermeneutics of Christian narrative, theology and ethics are two sides of the same coin. Theological reflection that does not lead to questions about Christian moral decisions in both the personal and social realms of life is not theological reflection about Christian faith. And any form of Christian ethics that does not look for guidance to the doctrines and symbols contained in Christian narrative may be a form of morality but not really a "Christian" ethic.[54]

While acknowledging that attention to biblical narrative has led some Christian communities into a sectarian ethic of withdrawal from the world, Stroup maintains that Christian narrative requires an ethic in which Christ is understood to be, in H. Richard Niebuhr's classic description, the "transformer of culture." Christian discipleship is seen as a costly engagement with the world in anticipation of the coming Kingdom.

Christian narrative, which includes but is by no means limited to biblical narrative, cannot be expected to furnish prescriptive answers to the question of what is to be done in situations of moral choice.

> The confessional narratives of the Christian community only provide the context in which ethical questions are asked and answered. . . .

Christian narrative simply provides the moral posture or disposition the Christian community assumes in relation to its larger social
world, and Christian narrative provides the [theological] symbols
and [ethical] principles by which the community responds to moral
issues.[55]

As will be evident in the next chapter, this summarizes a view that is
widely held. However, because of Stroup's moving back and forth between
the categories of 'biblical' and 'Christian' narrative (as in the preceding
paragraph), it is not clear whether Stroup thinks that scripture itself
commends ethical principles or that they emerge from the Christian
community's response to biblical narrative. Thus, the precise relation
between ethical principles, the non-narrative portions of scripture, and
biblical narrative remains unspecified.

CONCLUSION

Any attempt to assess the significance of a recent and ongoing discussion
must be provisional. Further work by the participants may clarify present
ambiguities or move forward in new and unexpected directions. It is
already clear, however, that the current attention to narrative serves to
refocus theology toward the church and its scripture. For this reason,
narrative is a welcome feature of current methodological discussion. Construing the Bible as narrative can facilitate the theological appropriation of
scripture. Furthermore, it is a use of scripture that is less arcane and more
accessible to laypersons than some widely practiced alternatives. Continuity between second-order theological discourse and the liturgy and popular piety of the church is a beneficial by-product of reading biblical texts or
the Bible as a whole as narrative.

The postliberal-particularistic, Barthian reading of biblical narrative
described by Frei is by far the most promising approach to "narrative
theology." When theology is considered the self-description of the Christian cultural-linguistic community, narrative provides conceptual tools for
displaying distinctive features of scripture and the Christian tradition.
Biblical narrative is seen to depict a world that is at once the world of the
story and the world of our everyday existence. As the Christian community's
self-description, theology is, in Frei's terms, the "conceptual redescription"
of the world of biblical narrative in belief and life.

Does the postliberal view of narrative convert theology into a ghetto language unintelligible to outsiders? That is precisely what its critics fear. They want theological arguments to be based on evidence accessible to Christians and non-Christians alike. To facilitate communication beyond the faith community, they seek a religion-neutral, putatively more public idiom in which to express the claims of Christianity.[56] Moreover, they are eager to prove before the bar of public rationality that such claims are not only meaningful but true. If one is going to talk about biblical narrative, they say, it had better be in the context of a universal hermeneutics.

The fear that postliberal theology cannot communicate outside the pulpit or church basement is unwarranted. For theology to find a "conversable" voice does not require that it first be translated into a religious Esperanto.[57] Nobody speaks that way, and if anyone were to try, few would care enough to listen. A postliberal approach to narrative is at no disadvantage when it comes to conversing in a culture that is, after all, less secular than sometimes imagined. Neither is postliberal theology unintelligible to the academic community. As I have indicated, social scientists, historians, and literary critics are quite accustomed to viewing religious traditions and texts along the lines of the cultural-linguistic model. Indeed, one of the model's strengths is that it obviates any theological need for a defensive posture toward these disciplinary perspectives. A conversable postliberal theology will not persuade or convert all of its conversation partners, but neither will it baffle them. Comprehension does not require confession.

Controversy about narrative between liberal-universalistic and postliberal-particularistic theologians may be seen as the latest round in the perennial debate on the proper relation between apologetic and dogmatic theology. It may be granted that each has its place and, perhaps, its own methods and standards. Still, one may suspect that a good, conversable dogmatics is the best apologetics.[58] It may not be fruitful, however, to continue to argue about narrative methodology. As one of the principals observes, "The proof of the pudding is in the tasting, and so the time has come to stop talking about descriptive [postliberal, narrative] theology and start engaging in it."[59]

Nevertheless, even if narrative's central importance as a theological category were to be acknowledged universally, problems would remain. 'Narrative' is not a universal solvent for all theological disagreements. In the first place, attention to different narratives within scripture may yield discrepant conclusions. Second, the same narrative or biblical narrative as a whole can be construed in different ways and used to warrant a variety of substantive theological proposals. Although the plurality of readings is not infinite—at least where the church and a confessional interpretive tradition are accorded authority—it is ineradicable. In the face of theological disagreement, it will not suffice to dismiss differing opinions as being insufficiently grounded in narrative when, in fact, they may simply be grounded in alternative readings. When the distinction between reading and readings is unheeded, theological argument cannot be incisive. While not always providing unanimous answers to theological questions, attention to narrative can show us where to look.

6

THE PLACE OF BIBLICAL
NARRATIVE IN CHRISTIAN ETHICS

It is widely assumed that biblical narrative ought to inform and shape
Christian belief and life. Doubtless, scripture has been influential and in
some quarters continues to be. However, it must be recognized that today
many Christians are biblically illiterate. As one observer puts it:

> There is now a widespread unfamiliarity in the church with what
> were at one time old and familiar names and stories in scripture. . . . It
> is also a mystery to many people what the Bible has to do with life
> in the twentieth century. Even many of those individuals in the
> church who know something of the content of scripture do not
> understand how to apply it to their personal and social existence.[1]

The factors contributing to this state of affairs are many and diverse. But
certainly one of them is the fact that many of those whose professional task
is to scrutinize, interpret, and pass on the tradition are themselves unsure
about the relation between the community's scripture and its vision of the
moral life.

A few seem ready to declare the Christian community's independence
from scriptural influence:

> The ethical positions of the New Testament are the children of
> their own times and places, alien and foreign to this day and age.

Amidst the ethical dilemmas which confront us, we are now at
least relieved of the need or temptation to begin with Jesus, or the
early church, or the New Testament, if we wish to develop coherent ethical positions. We are freed from bondage to that tradition, and we are able to propose . . . that tradition and precedent
must not be allowed to stand in the way of what is humane and
right.[2]

Nevertheless, as I have argued in earlier chapters, it is folly to suppose that
one stands or makes moral judgments apart from *some* tradition. Moreover,
most moral theologians (indeed, I suspect, most Christians) continue to
believe that scripture ought to exert *some* influence on the moral lives of
those who understand themselves to be members of that tradition and
community. The crucial question is not so much whether there will be
influence but what sort of influence it should be.

Many Christian thinkers seem to have despaired of stating—except in
the vaguest of terms—what relation should obtain between scripture and
ethics. Numerous reasons could be cited to explain how such a foundational
matter came to be seen as problematic. One oft-cited reason is that, for the
most part, biblical scholars have neglected to focus their attention on the
ethics of scripture (either the ethics of the various groups and authors or
some sort of amalgamation). At the same time, Christian ethicists have
often ignored scripture or have merely exploited it as a source of literary
allusions. Consequently, until quite recently, there has been relatively
little serious conversation between the disciplines of biblical studies and
theological ethics.

In this chapter, I shall take up the long-neglected "problem" of scripture
and ethics. After identifying problematic features of "the ethics of scripture"
and "the relation between scripture and ethics" as they are discussed in
the writings of biblical scholars, I shall survey the traditional ways in which
scripture has been employed within Christian ethics. Then, some recent
constructive proposals as to the role scripture ought to play in theological
ethics will be explored. Finally, I shall examine the claim that the construal
of scripture as narrative offers a way of specifying how scripture is and
ought to be normative in shaping Christian moral life.

It has been suggested that there now exists a consensus among biblical
scholars and Christian ethicists to the effect that, while "Christian ethics is
not synonymous with biblical ethics, . . . the Bible is (somehow) normative
for Christian ethics."[3] Yet biblical scholars have been quick to point out

the difficulties attendant on the notion that there is a "biblical ethic" or "ethics" in any modern sense of the term. Furthermore, they have counseled caution in attempting to relate the Bible to contemporary ethical discussions. Before jumping into the problem of scripture and ethics, it is useful to recognize that this inquiry is a species of biblical theology and is thus encumbered by some of the liabilities of its genus.

PROBLEMS OF BIBLICAL THEOLOGY

In his influential article "Contemporary Biblical Theology," Krister Stendahl observes that the fundamental tension in the discipline of New Testament theology lies between the twin goals of understanding what a text *meant* in the situation of its origin and what, if anything, it *means* to the modern reader.[4] While the historical descriptive task is enormously difficult and complex in itself, the pivotal question regards the relationship between the theological (what it means) and descriptive (what it meant) tasks.[5] Stendahl reckons it to be mutually advantageous for historians and theologians to respect this distinction with circumspection. Such an approach encourages historians to attend to the historical particularity of various texts and to refrain from rushing too quickly to theological conclusions (or presuppositions) that can prejudge, distort, or constrain the text as it stands. Patient historical scholarship can help to shape and correct erroneous theological understandings, even those as entrenched as Augustine's and Luther's interpretation of Romans 7.[6] Stendahl believes that his proposal is validated in the pulpit of the church, where the preacher "translates" biblical modes and patterns of thought in the "language" of the contemporary setting, seeking to present the Bible "in its original intention and intensity, as an ever new challenge to thought, faith, and response."[7]

However fruitful this might be, the terms of Stendahl's classic distinction are not easily kept. In the first place, no historical scholarship can be "objective" in any absolute sense. The finitude of the historian, the fact that what constitutes an "event" must be based on a logically prior, ahistorical discrimination or judgment, the antiquity of the texts, and the relative scarcity of contemporary sources combine to make a purely descriptive recovery of "what it meant" highly problematic. Second, even if the descriptive task were to be successful (by whatever historical methodology), "*whether* the results of exegesis are relevant [to theology], and *what* patterns in scripture are studied in exegesis depend on a logically prior and imaginative decision about how to construe scripture which is not itself corrigible by the results of any kind of biblical study."[8] Such considerations serve to complicate the tasks of identifying the ethics (plural) of scripture and of "translating" the biblical witness into contemporary idioms.

THE ETHICS OF SCRIPTURE

J. L. Houlden is one biblical scholar who has attended to the ethical materials within scripture. His approach is one that does not violate in any way the canons of modern New Testament study. Sensitive to the variety of ethical perspectives in scripture, Houlden resists the notion that there is such a thing as "*the* New Testament view." Instead, he carefully distinguishes one writer from another and tries to show the part that ethics played in their respective theological views.[9]

Houlden's general conclusion is that ethics, understood in the modern sense of an independent, autonomous concern for human aims and conduct, plays a minimal role in the thought world(s) of the New Testament. Several major religious forces, operative to a greater or lesser extent in the various New Testament communities of authorship, served to circumscribe the realm of the ethical. Houlden lists (1) the devaluing of the material world, (2) the expectation of the imminent end of the world, (3) the view that character and conduct are to conform to the example of God and Jesus or (4) to divine commands, and, finally, (5) the idea of justification by faith as factors inhibiting attention to ethics as an autonomous human concern.[10]

These "religious forces," it must be noted, should not be considered peripheral obstacles to be overcome. Indeed, they may be central to Houlden's enterprise. Wayne A. Meeks, in his presidential address to the Society of Biblical Literature, argues that, to understand the moral universe of the first Christian groups, one must discover "how their symbolic universe worked." This requires the adoption of George Lindbeck's cultural-linguistic model of religion. One cannot assume that ethics was for them what it is for us and then focus on those bits and pieces that seem to fit the bill. Instead, one must "attempt to describe the ethos of the larger culture — with its various local permutations — within which the Christian movement began and spread."[11] Such a sociology-of-knowledge approach is a difficult, yet necessary, undertaking that vastly complicates any simple, direct recovery of the ethics of early Christian communities.

Houlden, however, is confident that "concern with behavior in the world is a genuinely Christian concern, for the world is God's creation, and the forces which in the first century threatened to minimize and even abolish that concern could not be permitted to triumph in a faith resting on that foundation." Thus, he does not lament the fact that "our present-day Christian ethics are much more autonomous and much more apt to be argued on grounds of social or individual utility than the ethics of the New Testament." Christians today should not look to the New Testament for *direct* guidance. Rather, they should approach moral problems by asking, "On the basis of what we know of God through Christ, what should we now do?"[12]

This approach is warranted, not only with respect to problems on which scripture is silent (e.g., genetic engineering), but also where the Bible seems to speak with ongoing relevance, as in the command to love our neighbors as ourselves. One ought not simply ignore the cultural gap between the first century and the present or the fact that the New Testament authors themselves did not purport to be adjudicating moral questions for all people and all time. Houlden argues that "to be true to the deepest convictions of the leading New Testament writers, and more, to be faithful to the Lord who lay behind them, we need to be emancipated from the letter of their teaching," and to appropriate "centuries of Christian and non-Christian experience including . . . techniques in the human sciences."[13] Thus, contemporary Christians may or may not arrive at the same conclusion (with respect to some moral problem) as did their spiritual forebears. But whatever they decide, their conclusion must be the result of applying the same fundamental faith in a fresh setting. Cognizant of the ways in which scripture shapes the fundamental attitudes and convictions of Christians, Houlden suggests that

> the New Testament, like great art, may act upon a man to lead him to goodness, not by direct command but by a subtle and complex interaction which involves the New Testament writers' integrity, and behind them the impulses of Jesus, and the reader's readiness to create afresh out of the material of his own existence.[14]

While scripture does not provide a static moral code, it does remind contemporary Christians that morality pertains to human existence as it stands in relation to God.

Victor Paul Furnish is another biblical scholar who has written extensively on the ethics of scripture. Like Houlden, Furnish denies that scripture should be viewed as a source for solutions to the ethical problems of all subsequent ages. Both the moral problems and the "solutions" of the early Christians belong to the first century and are not necessarily transferable to the twentieth. Furnish agrees that "what is most important for us is an understanding of what the theological bases were upon which the earliest church's ethical teaching was founded and the way it went about interpreting and applying its gospel in daily life." With respect to the latter task, Furnish thinks that St. Paul's practice illustrates what James Gustafson has described as "a dialectic between more intuitive moral judgments and both scriptural and non-scriptural values . . . , a dialectic between principles of judgment which have a purely rational justification and which also appeal to the tradition expressed in scripture and developed in the Christian community." Thus, Christian moral reflection is located in the context of a community that understands itself "as from the beginning the creation of God's love and the recipient of his command to love."[15]

Furnish's analysis of St. Paul's moral teachings is helpful in that he locates the apostle's positions in the thought world of the first century and the local situations of the churches he addressed. Furnish shows that it is a mistake to assume that, just because the general *topics* Paul addressed (divorce, homosexuality, etc.) are the same as those under discussion today, the *issues* are the same. In virtually every case, Furnish shows that the current issues are significantly different from those Paul confronted. Nevertheless, the ongoing significance of Paul's instruction lies "in the underlying concerns and commitments" it reveals. Furnish maintains that Paul's teaching shows us "faith being enacted in love, and love seeking to effect its transforming power in the midst of the present age."[16]

Of course, there is often more than one passage of scripture relevant to a particular moral issue. Thus, the historical task of situating the texts is expansive. Yet, even when all of the relevant passages are properly understood, there remains the problem of how to evaluate and selectively apply biblical perspectives when they differ. The fact that the Bible does not always speak with one voice vastly complicates any attempt to seek theological or moral guidance from scripture.

One biblical scholar who has addressed this issue is Brevard Childs. Finding no system or technique within scripture for moving from the general imperatives of the Law of God to specific application within concrete situations, Childs suggests "a process of disciplined theological reflection that takes its starting point from the ethical issue at stake along with all its ambiguities and social complexities and seeks to reflect on the issue in conjunction with the Bible, which is seen in its canonical context." This is not an overtly biblicistic use of scripture. Non-theological considerations may play a major role in setting up the problem and the issues. Once this is done, the biblical theologian should "attempt to sketch the *full range* of the biblical witnesses within the canonical context which have bearing on the subject at issue." Thus, a selective and arbitrary use of scripture is avoided, and the variety of biblical voices are allowed to speak. As a second step, the theologian should "seek to understand the *inner movement* of the various witnesses along their characteristic axes when approached from within the context of the canon."[17] The result may be "a dynamic grid within the normative tradition" that offers "warrants" for deciding particular issues.

Where there appears to be a plurality of scriptural warrants, the theologian is well advised to consider each of them before selecting the one that seems most appropriate in the specific historical situation. The warrant should not be regarded as "an infallible rule of thumb, nor as an instance of an eternal principle, but as a time-conditioned testimony to God's will in which word the Christian seeks to discern afresh his own obedient action in a new historical movement." When the variety and status of the warrants are correctly understood, Childs recognizes that "Christians may disagree radically with one another on a particular course of action, and yet both positions may rightly appeal to some biblical warrant. . . . It is the primary task of the church to hold together the dissenting factions in Christian love."[18] Individual Christians, therefore, ought to be modest about the status of their discernment and to recognize that all human well-doing stands under God's judgment and ultimately must appeal to God's mercy.

In the preceding discussion, I have attempted to identify a few of the conclusions of recent biblical scholarship regarding the ethics of scripture and their applications in contemporary Christian ethics. Now let us see what Christian ethicists have to say about the appropriation of scripture for ethics.

TRADITIONAL USES OF SCRIPTURE IN ETHICS

Before turning to the question of how scripture ought to be used in theological ethics, it is instructive to survey some of the traditional ways in which scripture has been appropriated. James Gustafson, in an influential methodological study, sketches a typology of the ways in which the Bible has been employed.[19] As in all typologies, the categories are somewhat "ideal" and individuals may "fit" within more than one type. Nevertheless, the schema presents a useful map of the territory. Applying Kelsey's analysis, Gustafson recognizes that any use of scripture in ethics rests upon a prior determination as to how to bring coherence to the "meaning" of scripture's witness.[20] Some construe scripture as "revealed morality" offering authoritative guidance for judgment and behavior. Others conceive of it as "revealed reality," the "revelation of theological principles that are used to interpret what 'God is doing,' and thus, in turn, to give clues to what man as a moral agent is to do in particular historical circumstances."[21] He regards both conceptions as legitimate and thinks that no "sharp line" can be drawn between them. His essay seeks to illustrate the character of both types.

Gustafson separates uses of scripture falling under the "revealed morality" category into four subtypes. The first subtype holds that scripture reveals (directly) individual and communal actions that violate God's law and are to be judged wrong. Here, "the idea of moral law becomes the principle for ethical interpretation." Adherents to this view may have very different conceptions of the content of moral law and of its mode of application. Edward Long points out that Wycliffe, Calvin, contemporary fundamentalists, and, interestingly, some theological "liberals" all use the Bible in this way. Moreover, he suggests that to construe scripture as moral law is not necessarily to succumb to legalism or code morality. According to Long, Calvin's use of the Bible and C. H. Dodd's interpretation of Jesus' and Paul's perspective on first-century Judaism exemplify non-legalistic readings of scripture understood as moral law.

Gustafson's second subtype utilizes what it sees as moral ideals commended in scripture to evaluate human action. Long illustrates how the life and teachings of Jesus have been understood to warrant the promulgation of moral ideals or principles such as "the infinite values of the human soul" (Harnack) and "the impossible possibility of disinterested, sacrificial love" (Reinhold Niebuhr). While, as in the latter case, there is no sharp or "in-principle" distinction between biblical and rational or social scientific contributions toward understanding human problems, the role of biblical prescriptions (understood as ideals or principles) is never eliminated from moral reflection. As in the moral-law subtype, there is internal variation in the way the content of the ideals is specified, and again there is variety in the modes of application (How much compromise is tolerable? How much is necessary?). Furthermore, it is less clear that the language of moral ideals is as intrinsic to scripture as is the language of law. Different defenders of the moral-ideal model may make their cases in different ways.

The third subtype is an analogical method that judges actions to be wrong "which are similar to actions judged to be wrong or against God's will under similar circumstances in scripture, or are discordant with actions judged to be right or in accordance with God's will in scripture."[22] Such attempts to draw analogies between present and biblical events are notoriously difficult to control. The looseness of this method may be seen in Karl Barth's use of christological analogies in his political ethics. How can one persuasively establish that the events are similar? Which events are to be selected? Gustafson echoes Kelsey in observing that some prior ethical commitment is likely to determine the choice. If a strongly held position regarding some present event is the controlling factor, then a biblical "analogy" will be selected arbitrarily simply to "proof-text" one's ascriptural judgment. If, on the other hand, scripture is the controlling factor, then how is the similarity of a present event to be established?

It is a fourth subtype that Gustafson judges to be most adequate. Here, no single principle of ethical interpretation is distilled from the Bible:

> Scripture witnesses to a great variety of moral values, moral norms and principles through many different kinds of biblical literature. . . . The Christian community judges the actions of persons and groups to be morally wrong, or at least deficient, on the basis of reflective discourse about present events in the light of appeals to this variety of material as well as to other principles and experiences. Scripture is one of the informing sources for moral judgments, but it is not sufficient in itself to make any particular judgment authoritative.[23]

Obviously, questions about what controls one's reflection are as pertinent to this model as they were to the third. However, this "great variety" approach has the virtue of honestly acknowledging the ambiguity that surrounds all attempts to relate biblical norms, values, or concepts to contemporary situations. In fact, only the extremes of regarding the Bible as a straightforward collection of divine statutes or as an antique entirely irrelevant for ethical reflection seem to be excluded. Even as the "great variety" model agrees with Childs that a single focus is illegitimate, it recognizes along with Kelsey that some discrimination is ultimately inevitable.

Of course, scripture is often employed in a less specifically moral and more theological fashion. In Gustafson's typology, this is the view that construes the Bible as "revealed reality." Long calls this the "response model" because it regards the Bible as the record of the relationship between God and human persons and conceives of ethics as the response of the believing community to the activity of God. Discerning how God speaks or acts in human history is more a matter of creative intuition regarding relations and functions than of identifying precepts, principles, or laws.

This discernment of divine activity is a complex enterprise that may or may not be carried out with much explicit reference to scripture. Good examples of a theologian attempting to discern "what God is doing" in contemporary situations and events are H. Richard Niebuhr's essays "War as the Judgment of God," "Is God in the War?" and "War as Crucifixion." Naturally, scripture itself provides a great variety of "data" out of which one must formulate some generalization about God's disposition and action. Again, theologians may propose diverse thematizations such as liberation (Cone), crucifixion-resurrection (Shaull), hope (Moltmann), humanization (Lehmann), or the traditional Lutheran conceptions of law-gospel and orders of creation. Once this theological determination is made, there remains the problem of how to evaluate particular events and actions. Often, as in Lehmann's case, this is done by means of a kind of moral intuitionism in which the theonomous conscience of the Christian perceives what is right or good (i.e., that which is humanizing). Intuitionism, whether in theological or philosophical dress, leaves everything to the eye of the beholder.

To be sure, there are other theological users of scripture who want to give a more determinate shape to Christian moral reasoning. In either case, however, the explicitly moral teachings of scripture are employed only insofar as they cohere with the prior theological determination as to how to construe the Bible as a whole. While they are thus relegated to a secondary role, they are not necessarily ignored. Barth, for example, believes that they indicate the "prominent lines" or continuity of God's will for persons, even if they may not be regarded as laws, ideals, or unexceptionable rules. Gustafson's delineation of the traditional "types" is not intended to draw "sharp lines" between the several uses of scripture, nor to anathematize any of the models.

SOME CONSTRUCTIVE PROPOSALS

A significant Roman Catholic perspective on these issues is presented in Charles Curran's "Dialogue with the Scriptures: The Role and Function of the Scriptures in Moral Theology."[24] Curran places himself squarely in the camp of those who conceive Christian ethics on a relational or responsibility model (although he does see some deontological and teleological considerations as being of secondary importance). He opposes the direct application of the Bible's moral teachings to contemporary problems and any arbitrarily selective appeals to texts. While he maintains that scripture always requires interpretation, he warns against the exclusive employment of selective thematizations such as liberation. Curran raises two methodological questions that are important for the present discussion. The first concerns the relation between the methodology of Christian ethics and that of non-Christian, philosophical or human ethics in general. He rejects the claims of Barth and Lehmann that Christian ethics must be methodologically distinctive (because it is based on revelation rather than reason). Instead, he opts for a methodology that is common to "the ethical enterprise" in general, as practiced by Christians and non-Christians alike.

Curran's second question becomes relevant at this point. What is the relation between biblical and non-biblical sources of ethical wisdom? Curran is emphatic that scripture cannot be the sole source for Christian ethics. In his view, Christian ethics is not particularly distinctive in either methodology or *content*: "Non-Christians can and do arrive at the same ethical conclusions and also embrace and treasure even the loftiest of proximate motives, virtues, and goals which Christians in the past have wrongly claimed only for themselves." Thus, Curran believes that he assumes less than even Gustafson about the distinctiveness of Christian ethics. Nevertheless, like Gustafson, Curran maintains that scripture plays a significant role in forming the "stance, horizon, and posture" and self-understanding of Christians. Scripture "allows us to reflect on who the Christian is and what his attitudes, dispositions, goals, values, norms, and decisions are" as they are shaped by the "Christian mysteries of creation, sin, incarnation, redemption, and resurrection destiny."[25]

Gustafson's normative preference, exhibited throughout his many writings, is to employ scripture theologically and to look for signs of what God is doing on the current scene. At the same time, as noted above, he suggests that any moral use of scripture be along the lines of what he called the "great variety" model. In his one constructive statement relating scripture and ethics, he argues that the Gospels can be related to the moral life by understanding their influence on the "sort of persons members of the community become." He does not claim that this is the only or even a sufficient way of relating the Gospels to morality, but rather that it is an important way. Quoting Sallie McFague, Gustafson maintains that the Gospels function in character formation in the way other literature does, by providing "concrete, varied, and creative depictions of the basic structure of human experience; they create a vision of life in relation to God, to the world, and to other persons."[26] Thus, the Gospels reorient the action, intention, and disposition of persons who attend to them. Gustafson does not understand this shaping by gospel paradigms to be a matter of strict analogical reasoning. Rather, Christians' "moral sensibilities" and "imaginations" are involved in the movement from gospel paradigms to specific actions in the world. Not only is this approach philosophically defensible in Gustafson's view, but it is also warranted by the New Testament itself (see Philippians 1:27 and 2:5).

While less open than Gustafson to moral uses of scripture, Thomas Ogletree is similarly concerned to emphasize the Bible's influence on Christian self-understanding. In a major constructive work deploying a hermeneutic informed by phenomenology, Ogletree seeks "to display our essential connection with what the biblical texts are saying by means of the constitutive structures of the life world." The Bible does not bequeath perpetually applicable ethical principles, much less paradigms for social, political, or economic life. Instead, it offers, according to Ogletree, something more fundamental: "matrices of experience" that reflect "the creative accomplishments of the early churches in working out patterns of common life as ordered communities of faith and love."[27]

In encounter with these matrices, Christian readers can realize a "fusion of horizons." Although they identify themselves as descendants of the early Christians, they do not attempt to speak about ethics as their ancestors did. Christian ethics must be a "historical contextualism," combining deontological, consequentialist, and perfectionist or aretaic patterns of thought, which looks through the biblical matrices in order to discover ways of being and acting appropriate for Christians today. Paradoxically, "to say the same thing as the texts, we must say something different, . . . suited to the different reality within which we live."[28] What must remain the same, however, is Christian commitment to a radically eschatological vision. No less than their forebears, contemporary Christians must live lives that resonate the impulses of the coming new age.

Curran, Gustafson, and Ogletree all refer to the Bible's role in shaping the self-understanding, character, outlook, horizon, or stance of individual Christians. This function of scripture is given particular emphasis in the writings of Stanley Hauerwas. According to Hauerwas, "the question of the moral significance of Scripture . . . [is] a question about what kind of community the church must be to make the narratives of Scripture central for its life." With Kelsey, he holds that scriptural authority and Christian community are correlative; neither can exist without the other. Nevertheless, to say that scripture is authoritative is not to assume that there is a single normative concept of scripture. Hauerwas agrees with Kelsey that theologians must make imaginative suggestions as to how best to construe scripture and that their judgments must be influenced by the community and its narrative. At the same time, he thinks that Kelsey "fails to do justice to the ways the Scripture morally shapes a community."[29] His reason for saying this remains obscure. It is not clear that Kelsey does or would disagree with what Hauerwas goes on to explain about the function of scripture. Hauerwas's concern is to emphasize that the uses of scripture in liturgy, preaching, and morality are diverse and not readily susceptible to a single characterization. I do not believe, however, that Kelsey's idea of the *discrimen* denies this diversity.

Hauerwas maintains that the Christian canon is "the classic model for the understanding of God." Its status does not rest exclusively on the decision of the early church, because the canonical writings satisfy "our craving for a perfect story which we feel to be true." "The Scripture functions as an authority for Christians precisely because by trying to live, think, and feel faithful to its witness they are more nearly able to live faithful to the truth." For Hauerwas, the most appropriate way to understand scripture is to regard it as a narrative, or story. Forbearing to select a single theme or concept by which to "unify" scripture, Hauerwas prefers to adopt Kelsey's suggestion that the Bible may be regarded as "one vast, loosely structured non-fiction novel" with minor and major subplots. "The narrative of scripture not only 'renders a character' but renders a community capable of ordering its existence appropriate to such stories."[30] Thus, the canon is a task and challenge for the church as it seeks to recall the stories of the past that are to shape its life in the present.

Hauerwas anticipates the objection that he has merely redescribed as "moral" aspects of scripture and processes of its development, while failing to explain what we are to do with the straightforwardly "moral" aspects of scripture. To this criticism, he makes two replies. First, he suggests that many of our intellectual problems with texts forbidding, for example, adultery or resistance to evil stem from "a profound unwillingness to have our lives guided by [them]."[31] Second, he claims that a narrative reading of scripture helps to prevent taking the explicit commands and teachings as universal rules or principles isolated from their proper narrative and theological context. He advocates critical examination and evaluation of each of the specific moral teachings and acknowledges that they may or may not be relevant in the present. However, it is clearly wrong in his view to treat the *Haustafeln* as principles for all people in all communities throughout time. Indeed, it is to be expected that those outside the Christian community will judge certain biblical injunctions to be unwarranted and highly inappropriate. Attention to the narrative character of scripture serves to remind the reader that the moral teachings are "reminders of the radical nature of the new community that [God has] called into existence."[32]

While it might be said that there is general agreement among ethicists that scripture's role in character formation has been neglected until quite recently, there are many who wonder whether the retrieval of this function is being overemphasized by its most ardent proponents. For example, James Childress judges that "several recent interpretations of how scripture functions have overemphasized some features of the moral life — vision and perspectives, images and metaphors, stories, loyalties, and character" to the point of underestimating or distorting "the role of Scripture in Christian moral deliberation and justification." Hauerwas is the specific target of this criticism, although it applies to a number of other thinkers as well. Gustafson is excused on the basis of his attention to deliberation and justification even as he emphasizes the role of the Gospels in shaping the Christian's perspective and character. Childress warns that "responsibility" should not be considered the sole image or mode of the moral life. This is especially the case because some proponents of "response" models (e.g., Lehmann) entirely exclude the processes of deliberation and justification. Part of the reason for this, Childress believes, is theologians' desire to avoid what they take to be an unseemly, legalistic casuistry. However, Childress claims that "it may be necessary to take the risk of legalism in order to offer an adequate interpretation of responsibility, for we and others have to answer for our actions in relation to standards and consequences."[33]

Important as aretaic and aesthetic categories may be in bringing us to recognize our obligations, Childress argues that they cannot provide, in themselves, justification for those obligations. For justification, principles and rules are absolutely necessary. The necessity of justification, in turn, is established on both philosophical and theological grounds: "Not only is there a reason-giving capacity; there is also a reason-giving necessity imposed by our responsibility to God, to self, and to others, including the Christian community." Childress thinks that those who seek a "dialogue" between the authority of scripture and non-scriptural authorities are on the right track but that they have not yet clarified "how principles and rules in or authorized by Scripture relate to the biblical perspective and to principles and rules of natural morality."[34]

Childress's own proposal for relating scripture and ethics is akin to Gustafson's "great variety" model, which refuses to reduce scripture's moral import to any single category. The variety of the biblical material is to be respected, and scripture may be construed as law, ideals, and as a source for analogical reasoning. However, Childress emphasizes that some of the Bible's moral statements must be construed as principles or rules. Here he seeks a broader understanding of "law" than is customary, for example, among fundamentalists. Childress suggests that it is important to think "in terms of principles that establish presumptions and burdens of proof for the moral life." These prescriptions are "always relevant." They establish "a *prima facie* case for a course of action." Some may turn out to be conclusive and absolute (e.g., do not commit murder, do not commit rape, and do not act cruelly), while others may be rebuttable in certain circumstances.[35]

In bending over backwards to avoid absolutes, Christian ethics, according to Childress, has lost its balance. His primary concern is to restore balance:

> The ethicist has a responsibility within the Christian community to direct attention to principles and rules that *constitute* obligations that may otherwise be overlooked and neglected. In addition, he or she should direct attention to biblical stories, images, and metaphors that may enable us to *recognize* obligations.[36]

Both foci are necessary for an adequate explication of the Christian moral life.

Even if (as Childress rightly insists) vision, virtue, and character are not all there is to Christian ethics, it remains the consensus of the authors I have discussed that the Bible does and should influence the formation of Christian character. Hauerwas and, to some extent, Gustafson suggest that this influence can be explicated fully only when scripture is construed as story, or narrative. In the remainder of this chapter, I shall consider the meaning and implications of this suggestion. What does it mean to speak of biblical narrative, and how might it shape the Christian moral life? To answer the first question, it is useful to consult the analyses of literary critics and scholars of biblical literature.

BIBLICAL NARRATIVE

The term "narrative" has been understood to refer to "all those literary works which are distinguished by two characteristics: the presence of a story and a storyteller."[37] Obviously, such a minimalistic definition allows many different sorts of materials to be classified as narrative. What all narratives have in common, according to Frank Kermode, is that they spring from a human need to bring the past and future into coherence (even if it is only illusory) with the present. "Men, like poets, rush 'into the middest,' in medias res, when they are born; they also die in mediis rebus, and to make sense of their span they need fictive concords with origins and ends, such as give meaning to lives and to poems."[38] Narratives reassure us by ordering time in such a way as to convey "the sense of an ending" that is ours as well as their own.

Without narratives our time is merely chronological; our experience chaotic and insignificant. Whatever order is achieved through narrative — Kermode thinks narratives are often far from perspicuous in this regard — it is an order that must be imposed from outside. Order is never immanent in human experience. Thus, Kermode seems to share my agnosticism concerning the "anthropological thesis" that our experience has an inherent narrative structure. We must be told something we cannot discover for and within ourselves. The Bible provides a clear illustration of this ordering function: "It begins at the beginning ('In the beginning . . . ') and ends with a vision of the end ('Even so, come, Lord Jesus'); the first book is Genesis, the last Apocalypse."[39]

Of course, ordering time and giving coherence and meaning to human existence are functions widely ascribed to religious worldviews and rituals. This functional similarity is one of the foci of the newly emergent discipline of religion and literature. One of its practitioners, Wesley Kort, defines narratives as "extended verbal expressions in prose which have for their primary intention the creation of images of setting, plot, character and tone." He observes that many modern narratives (such as Albert Camus's *Plague*, Graham Greene's *Burnt-Out Case*, Nathanael West's *Miss Lonelyhearts*, and Günter Grass's *Cat and Mouse* — to cite only a few of those he discusses) seem to "carry or imply religious or religiously suggestive meanings." This he attributes to the fact that "the elements of narrative [identified in his definition], particularly when reflected upon, naturally lead to, or draw to themselves, associations or complications which are religious or religiously important."[40] Setting suggests limitation and otherness; plot derives from ritual and the rehearsal of great events; character presents paradigmatic images of human possibilities; and tone conveys the experience of wholeness, affirmation, and belief.[41] Thus, Kort correlates elements of narrative with important characteristics of religion such that they stand in relation to each other like "two walls of a canyon . . . , separated but with structural matching points." "What fiction has in common with religion," according to Kort, "is a fund of resources to constitute an entire world."[42]

The way in which literary texts constitute and posit worlds is described in Erich Auerbach's classic work on the representation of reality in Western literature. Auerbach identifies some distinctive features of biblical narrative by contrasting the Homeric scene in which Odysseus is recognized by a scar on his thigh with the biblical account of the sacrifice of Isaac. Equally ancient and epic, these two stories are very different stylistically:

> The two styles, in their opposition, represent basic types: on the one hand fully externalized description, uniform illumination, uninterrupted connection, free expression, all events in the foreground, displaying unmistakable meanings, few elements of historical development and of psychological perspective; on the other hand, certain parts brought into high relief, others left obscure, abruptness, suggestive influence of the unexpressed, "background" quality, multiplicity of meanings and the need for interpretation, universal-historical claims, development of the concept of the historically becoming, and preoccupation with the problematic.[43]

Similarly, in the New Testament, St. Mark's recounting of Peter's denial following the arrest of Jesus does not fit into any antique genre. Auerbach observes that, in contrast to the static literature of Greco-Roman antiquity, New Testament narratives depict "a world which on the one hand is entirely real, average, identifiable as to place, time, and circumstances, but which on the other hand is shaken in its very foundations, is transforming and renewing itself before our eyes." As New Testament characters struggle with the impact of Jesus' teachings, personality, and fate, ordinary occurrences "assume the importance of world-revolutionary events, as later on they will for everyone."[44] What is striking about biblical narratives is the distinctive intermingling of the everyday and the extraordinary, the individual and the cosmic.

The characteristic features of biblical narrative are not limited to qualities of the texts themselves. According to Auerbach, the texts intend to grasp and hold their reader: "Far from seeking, like Homer, merely to make us forget our own reality for a few hours, [biblical narrative] seeks to overcome our reality; we are to fit our own life into its world, feel ourselves to be elements in the structure of universal history."[45] This is so because

> the world of the Scripture stories is not satisfied with claiming to be a historically true reality—it insists that the only real world is destined for autocracy. All other scenes, issues, and ordinances have no right to appear independently of it, and it is promised that all of them, the history of all mankind, will be given their due place within its frame, will be subordinated to it. The Scripture stories do not, like Homer's, court our favor, they do not flatter us that they may please and enchant us—they seek to subject us, and if we refuse to be subjected we are rebels.[46]

Thus, for Auerbach, biblical narratives mean to exert authority over and transform their readers' self-understanding.

Among those who read the Bible as narrative are a number of Old and New Testament scholars. Some focus their attention on specific narratives within scripture, while others read entire genres of biblical literature as narrative. For example, James Sanders writes: "The basic structure of the Pentateuch is not that of a law code but rather that of a narrative. The Torah is essentially a story of the origins of ancient Israel."[47] After surveying the various literary forms of the New Testament, Amos Wilder, in similar fashion, maintains that, of all genres, "narrative is uniquely impor-

tant to Christianity."[48] By "narrative," Wilder means to refer to both the
stories about Jesus and the stories or parables Jesus told.

However, as George Stroup observes, most contemporary students of
New Testament narrative do not speak of "narrative" in such a broad
way.[49] Followers of the later Heidegger, champions of what is known as the
"New Hermeneutic," and others argue that the parable is the quintessential
narrative form. They regard parables as metaphors "which rupture the
grip of tradition on man's apprehension of the world in order to permit a
glimpse of another world which is not really a different but a strangely
familiar world."[50] They reject the traditional practice of viewing the parables as allegories or stories that teach a moral lesson. Stroup faults this
"parable school" for their Heideggerian hypostatization of parabolic language and for their tendency to treat parables as if they were "self-
contained" and ahistorical. Because, in part, they ignore the historicality of
biblical narrative, their readings of the parables are "susceptible to whatever strong winds of interpretation happen to be blowing at the moment."[51]
Stroup finds a more promising approach to New Testament narrative in
the work of a second group of scholars, for whom the object of study is the
gospel form as a whole.[52] Here there are built-in checks on the tendency to
import extra-biblical meaning into the texts. This "gospel" approach pays
due regard to both the historical setting of the text within the early
Christian community and to what Auerbach regards as the text's claim to
represent universal history.

Study of the Gospels as narrative has become a growth industry.[53] In his
recent book *The Ethics of Mark's Gospel—In the Middle of Time*, Dan O.
Via, Jr., shifts from his earlier focus on parable to take in the literary form
of the gospel. Employing literary-critical and structuralist tools in a phenomenological method, Via exhibits Mark's conception of the Christian
life through an analysis of the Gospel's narrative form. Persuaded by
Hepburn, MacIntyre, and Hauerwas that narrative is necessary for understanding ethics, Via interprets Mark with an eye toward displaying the
connections with contemporary concerns. He believes that "the understanding of time is the one cardinal point at which New Testament ethics
and constructive ethics can meet."[54]

Via sides with Ricoeur and Crites against Kermode, maintaining that
the temporal structure of narrative corresponds with the structure of
human existence. Plot corresponds with reality. It is not an illusory imposi-
tion on life. Thus, Mark's narrative of life "between the times" can teach its
readers about discipleship in any age. Is it a lesson that can be learned only

from narrative? Via is "inclined to acquiesce in the view that narrative does not say anything *conceptually* that cannot be said otherwise." Yet he insists that narrative does make a unique contribution. Like Hepburn and contrary to Braithwaite, Via wants narratives to do more than simply fortify narrative-independent morality. Narratives, he says, "attract the attention and involvement of the reader by the informing of content and . . . create the sense of living the portrayed possibilities for existence in the course of time."[55] In Mark, one indispensable function of the narrative is to warn that the radical demands of the Kingdom are so arduous that the disciple should learn to persevere with no expectation of attaining perfection.

Still other professional and non-professional students of scripture look beyond the literary form of the gospel. They maintain that the whole Bible, for all its non-narrative passages, can be read as an immense, sprawling, nonfictional story. The principal character of the biblical "story" is God. The "story" discloses the identity and character of God as his intentions are enacted in the narrative. In similar fashion, the "story" illustrates paradigmatic human responses to God's action. As observed in the last chapter, Karl Barth and Hans Frei read biblical narrative in this way and use the "identity descriptions" (Kelsey) displayed in scripture to authorize their theological proposals. Stanley Hauerwas's somewhat similar appropriation of biblical narrative for theological ethics is the subject of the next chapter.

I now return to my second question: how might the Christian moral life be shaped if scripture were to be construed as narrative? Or, more precisely, what effects might a narrative construal of the Bible have on the problems of scripture and ethics treated above?

BIBLICAL NARRATIVE AND CHRISTIAN ETHICS

In terms of Gustafson's typology, scripture as narrative could be used in at least three ways. First, there could be a moral use of scripture as narrative of the analogical subtype. One might propose that Christians are to imitate the virtuous deeds of biblical characters and to reenact the biblical story or stories in their own lives. There is a suggestion of this possibility when Barth says:

> We are not only invited to be contemporaneous and like-minded with the biblical men. We are not only exhorted to hear the

command as they heard it. . . . The command given to them and
heard by them becomes directly the command given ,to us and to
be heard by us. Their task becomes our task.[56]

However, this use of scripture is highly problematic.

In the first place, as Gustafson says, it is difficult to see how the analogies
between the biblical situations and our own are to be controlled. Second,
what is to be done when no biblical analogy is apparent? Are Christians
bereft of guidance in the face of radically new moral perplexities? Third,
this approach seems to disrespect the autonomy and freedom of the moral
agent. Suppose one can identify an appropriate biblical analogy. Is the
Christian simply to act as the biblical characters do in the story? Such
mimicry would diminish the autonomy of the moral agent and the freedom in which Christians are to act on behalf of their neighbors. Barth
himself, while maintaining that Christians are to fit themselves into the
world of biblical narrative, nevertheless warns that Christians are not to
attempt to impersonate or imitate the people of the Bible in *what* they
did. Rather, they are to emulate the obedience in which the biblical
characters respond to divine commands directed to them as individuals in
their specific time and place. Finally, the analogical use tends to render the
Christian moral life an extended exercise in role-playing that would require
an unusual capacity for imaginative identification if the actors are not to
remain alienated from their roles. In any event, this kind of artificial
performance is something very different from the biblically mandated,
profound reorientation of the self toward love of God and neighbor.

The second possible use of scripture as narrative would be a moral use
encompassing all four of Gustafson's subtypes (moral law, ethical, analogical,
and "great variety"). Here, narrative could serve as an interpretive context
for the variety of moral teachings in scripture. Childress insists that non-
narrative moral materials not be ignored, and Hauerwas suggests that they
may be understood and used correctly only when they are located within
the narrative framework. Even so, all of the problems identified above
(selection of texts, control of analogies, status of non-biblical sources)
would remain as before. While it may be true that attention to the
narrative context might serve as a hedge against misinterpreting explicit
moral teachings, just as Gustafson's "great variety" model may protect
against reductive appropriations of biblical materials, it would not be a
radically new approach to the use of scripture in ethics.

A third option would be to reject all moral uses of scripture and instead to regard biblical narrative as a specification of the post-ethical or theological use of the Bible along the "relation-response" lines favored by Gustafson, Curran, and Ogletree. Yet this option is not without difficulties. How are the Ten Commandments, the Beatitudes, the love command, and other non-narrative moral teachings to be incorporated into the story? Second, the problem of other sources is not addressed. Moreover, the problem of other sources is not simply external to the appropriation of biblical narrative. It arises, not only after the reading of scripture, but in the reading as well.

As I explained earlier, any attempt to summarize the biblical plot, describe its characters, or construe its message involves selective judgments about the relative importance and reciprocal interpretation of various texts. Is there to be a "canon within the canon"? On what authority and criteria might it be established? No doubt some, including some narrativists of the liberal-universalistic school, would like to see the canon opened or its authoritative status diminished. Other stories, they might say, reflect the narrative quality of human experience and edify their readers as much as or more than certain biblical stories. Why not allow all the stories to be heard? That the concept of a canon is under assault in literary circles exacerbates the problem.

Moreover, even where there is agreement on the texts to be considered, the interpretation of scripture is a notoriously diverse enterprise. Of necessity, one reads through the lenses of some theological or philosophical tradition. How are diverse alien readings through Freudian, Marxian, phenomenological, structuralist, or semiotic lenses to be evaluated? If they are not to be welcomed, how can they be excluded? The project of construing scripture as narrative does not escape these issues.

The theologian who aspires to employ biblical narrative may face a formidable challenge from the narrative itself. According to Kermode, narratives deliberately conceal "secrets." Commenting on Jesus' enigmatic sayings concerning the parables of the Kingdom, recorded in the fourth chapter of Mark's gospel, Kermode observes:

> Only those who already know the mysteries—what the stories really mean—can discover what the stories really mean. As a matter of fact, the teacher . . . showed himself irritated with his elect for seeking explanations of what they already, in principle, knew. And, if we are to believe Mark, they continued to be slow learners, prone to absurd error. But they did know that even plain stories mean more than they seem to say, that they may contain mysteries

inaccessible to all but privileged interpreters—and perhaps not always with any great measure of certainty even to them.[57]

To get beyond the surface or "carnal" sense of the text and to grasp its hidden or "spiritual" sense, one must pry into the narrative's secrets. This prying, or "overreading," is bound to yield a plurality of interpretations because of "the capacity of narrative to submit to the desires of this or that mind without giving up [its] secret potential."[58]

Could this pluralism have been intended or, at least, envisioned by the biblical authors and editors? Whoever they were, they could hardly have been in a position to exert tight control over the interpretation of their readers. "Unless, of course," as Michael Walzer wryly suggests, "the author is God: but God has obviously chosen not to exercise close control, and we must assume, along with one of the central strands of Jewish interpretation, that He intends all the meanings that He has made us capable of discovering."[59] In Christian communities where a confessional or other interpretive tradition specifies a normative reading, the problems of narrative opacity and plural interpretation are mitigated. Nevertheless, construing scripture as narrative does not resolve all of the persistent difficulties attendant to the relation of scripture and ethics.

7

NARRATIVE, VIRTUE, AND CHARACTER: A THEOLOGICAL PROPOSAL

To what extent is narrative a heuristically useful category for theological ethics? This is the inquiry of the book as a whole and the precise focus of this chapter. I shall examine the work of Stanley Hauerwas, who is, in my judgment, the most significant and influential exponent of narrative among contemporary Christian ethicists. My choice of Hauerwas as the representative theological figure is justified further by the fact that he is allied with one of the principal representative philosophers, Alasdair MacIntyre, discussed in earlier chapters.[1] As suggested at the outset, the uses of narrative and the attendant problems among philosophical and theological ethicists are analogous. Thus, the philosophical issues pertaining to freedom, rules, and relativism will reappear in my critical discussion of Hauerwas's views. I shall say nothing more here about those religious writers who speak of narrative as biography or autobiography, for reasons that are, I trust, tolerably clear in Chapter 5.

Hauerwas's two book-length studies and five volumes of collected essays are an attempt to move beyond Christian (especially, Protestant) ethics' recent legacy of subjectivism and occasionalism by restoring virtue and character to a place of prominence. Throughout these writings, it is clearer what Hauerwas opposes than proposes. However, enough of his constructive views are visible to warrant the critical scrutiny offered here. I shall begin with a brief sketch of some of his major themes. By posing some theological questions, I shall clarify Hauerwas's position in relation to other theological treatments of narrative. Then I shall return to those recurring philosophical issues. Once Hauerwas's general program has been examined, I shall discuss his understanding of the church's social-ethical task. In the next and final chapter, I shall observe the way in which his narrative perspective regards certain social-ethical issues concerning marriage and family. There his proposals will serve as a test case for the importance of narrative.

HAUERWAS'S CONSTRUCTIVE ACCOUNT

To begin, *Character and the Christian Life* is a sustained criticism of the divine command–human obedience metaphor employed by Barth, Bultmann, and many other Protestants in subsequent decades:

> The language of command tends to be inherently occasionalistic with a correlative understanding of the self that is passive and atomistic. The self that is justified is the self at this time and in this place but not the self which has any duration or growth. As a result, there seems to be no aspect of our experience that makes intelligible the theological affirmations associated with the doctrine of sanctification.[2]

While holding that a revival of the categories of virtue and character is necessary in order to preserve the intelligibility of sanctification, Hauerwas does not want to compromise historicist assumptions by falling back into a theory of natural law. Instead, he turns to recent Anglo-American philosophy of mind. There he finds the resources to defend a conception of character as "the qualification of a man's self-agency through his beliefs, intentions and actions, by which a man acquires a moral history befitting his nature as a self-determining being."[3] By using the metaphor of character, Hauerwas hopes to satisfy the requirements of traditional Christian theology while, at the same time, conforming to our everyday use of the word "character" in ordinary moral discourse.

For Hauerwas, it is axiomatic that ethical analysis must proceed from the moral agent's own perspective on his or her actions rather than from the perspective of an "ideal observer." Nor are particular moralities to be measured according to allegedly universal, necessary criteria for moral rationality. Hauerwas maintains that, in order to assess the action of a particular moral agent, one must begin by attending to the distinctive features of his or her overall vision of life. Only after one has uncovered the particular moral notions embedded in the agent's perspective or worldview can one go on to consider patterns of action and to make judgments about the coherence or incoherence of a particular action with the character of the agent. Hence, "vision" appears as another important category in Hauerwas's program.

His overarching objective is to call attention to the particularity of the Christian moral life. The Christian ethic is "a qualified ethic." It is not "a universal ethic."[4]

> We neither are nor should we be formed primarily by the publicly defensible rules we hold, but by the stories and metaphors through which we learn to intend the variety of our existence. Metaphors and stories suggest how we should see and describe the world— that is how we should "look-on" our selves, others and the world—in ways that rules taken in themselves do not. Stories and metaphors do this by providing the narrative accounts that give our lives coherence.[5]

For Hauerwas, the distinctiveness of Christian morality is a function of the Christian story, or narrative, which provides the metaphors, categories, and concepts that determine vision and shape Christian character. Thus, character, vision, and narrative emerge as the central themes of Hauerwas's perspective on Christian ethics.

The relations between these emphases and which one is to be the controlling feature are somewhat obscure. There is reason to think that Hauerwas considers character the conceptual center of his thought: "Christian ethics is best understood as an ethics of character."[6] However, as will be shown below, some of the claims Hauerwas makes on behalf of these three features seem to be incompatible.[7] Were Hauerwas to provide a more thorough and systemic account of his position than he has to date, I suspect that narrative would be identified as the dominant and controlling term.[8] In any event, even the present texts show narrative to be Hauerwas's central concern. It is narrative that focuses vision and forms character. Unfortunately, narrative itself is not defined with sufficient clarity.

THEOLOGICAL QUESTIONS

What, precisely, does Hauerwas mean by narrative? The answer to this question should provide an indication of whether he is working within an "experiential-expressive" or a "cultural-linguistic" model of religion as these are defined in Chapter 5. Hauerwas is aware that, in the theological literature under discussion, " 'story' is sometimes used as such an inclusive category it tends to be vacuous." How inclusive or exclusive is Hauerwas's own use of 'story'? On the one hand, he says that "there are aspects of our experience that make story unavoidable." Stephen Crites's claim that "a man's sense of his own identity seems largely determined by the kind of story he understands himself to have been enacting through the events of his career, the story of his life," is quoted with favor. Hauerwas also expresses his agreement with Sallie McFague's assertion that "we learn who we are through the stories we embrace as our own—the story of my life is structured by the larger stories (social, political, mythic) in which I understand my personal story to take place." According to Hauerwas, "stories are not just a literary genre . . . but a form of understanding that is indispensable" to self-understanding.[9] Thus, it appears that Hauerwas is committed to the general thesis regarding the narrative quality of human experience that coheres with an experiential-expressive conception of religion and theology.

On the other hand, Hauerwas also expresses an interest in narrative structure *per se*, which he describes as

> the connected description of action and of suffering which moves to a point. The point need not be detachable from the narrative itself. [In fact, it is better if there is no explicit *moral*.] The "point" . . . has to do with . . . the connected unfolding that we call *plot*; . . . a connection among elements (actions, events, situations) which is neither one of logical consequence nor one of mere sequence. The connection seems rather designed to move our understanding of a situation forward by developing or unfolding it. . . . What we demand of a narrative is that it display how occurrences are actions. Intentional behavior is purposeful not necessary. . . . It is the intentional nature of human action which evokes a narrative account.[10]

This use of narrative is reminiscent of Hans Frei's account of realistic narrative. Of course, Hauerwas's primary concern is not the description of certain formal features of biblical narrative. His purpose is to establish that narratives show the connectedness of intentional action and thus display character. As a Christian theologian, Hauerwas ultimately wants to illustrate the ways in which the stories told within the Christian community shape the lives and character of individual Christians. Neither of these purposes requires adherence to the general anthropological thesis. Indeed, they may be undermined or, at least, unnecessarily encumbered by it.

From time to time, Hauerwas seems to employ both the experiential-expressive and the cultural-linguistic models. There is talk about everyone having a story (as a function of self-understanding) in which the lines of authority in relation to scripture are unspecified, and there is talk of the Christian life as being the task of conforming one's own story to the biblical story. As I have suggested, the first seems to be in continuity with liberal Protestant universalism, while the second moves in a particularistic, postliberal, even Barthian direction. In view of his overarching interest in explaining the distinctiveness of the Christian moral life in conformity with the Christian story, it would seem that his purposes would be served best and most economically if he were to adhere scrupulously to the cultural-linguistic model and its cognate conception of theology as Christian self-description.

His most recent writings suggest that this is the direction in which he is now moving. For example, in *The Peaceable Kingdom* we are told that "Wittgenstein ended forever any attempt on my part to try to anchor theology in some general account of 'human experience.' "[11] Introducing *Against the Nations: War and Survival in a Liberal Age*, Hauerwas indicates that "the basic perspective" of the essays is consonant with Lindbeck's cultural-linguistic model of religion and with postliberal, intratextual theology. In fact, he identifies liberal theologians' allegiance to the experiential-expressive model as the justification for their erroneous belief that "there is a strong continuity between Christian and non-Christian morality."[12] That Hauerwas seems to have clarified his position is all to the good. However, there is little indication of what adjustments in his earlier views he is prepared to make in order to accommodate with consistency this narrowing of focus.[13]

Of course, to focus on biblical narrative as the revelation of God and his intentions for human beings is by no means to resolve all of the questions about the meaning of narrative. How is biblical narrative to be construed? In the preceding chapter, I observed that Hauerwas rejects the idea that the Bible contains any "revealed morality." He prefers to construe scrip-

ture as a narrative that "provides the resources necessary for the church to
be a community sufficiently truthful so that our conversation with one
another and God can continue across generations."[14] For Hauerwas, these
resources are the stories themselves and the ways in which their narrative
structures display character.[15] To construe any of the portions of scripture
as moral principles or rules, as James Childress insisted was necessary, is,
according to Hauerwas, to "betray the character of biblical literature" and
"to separate such an ethic from the understanding of salvation that makes
such an ethic intelligible in the first place."[16] Hauerwas and Childress
represent two antithetical positions regarding the relation between biblical
narrative and moral principles. In the former, biblical narrative excludes
principles or rules, and in the latter, biblical rules or principles are thought
to be integral to scripture.

Yet there seems to be a third, mediating position, which Hauerwas also
rejects. This view he characterizes as "biblical theology" in that it attempts
to identify certain themes and principles embedded in the narrative and
to reformulate them for use in ethics. Hauerwas considers Paul Ramsey to
be "a classical example of an ethicist exploiting the assumption that
biblical theology is primarily a matter of locating the central 'biblical'
concepts. Thus Ramsey stresses the centrality of love and covenant on the
assumption that in doing so his ethic is thereby 'biblical.' "[17] Hauerwas
fears that, when biblical ethics is construed in this way, covenant and love
become "abstractions" and "one wonders why appeals to scripture need to
be made at all, since one treats it as a source of general principles that once
in hand need no longer acknowledge their origins."[18]

In rejecting Hauerwas's characterization of his "method," Ramsey denies
that he has abstracted anything from scripture or sought to translate
scripture into a more general theological medium (for example, reason or
nature). He judges that "steadfast covenant love" is "nourished by the
shared memory of a particular community and firmly anchored precisely
in biblical narrative." Why, Ramsey asks, are covenant and love said to be
less biblical or less narratable biblically than the host of themes Hauerwas
introduces? Hauerwas has imposed "on other theologians a more rigorous
standard of justification of assumptions than on himself," and his exclusion of covenant and love from the narratable themes is arbitrary. Moreover,
it is not Ramsey's *stressing* these "concepts" (he would prefer not to call
them that) that *makes* them "biblical," any more "than Hauerwas' *stress* on
a multitude of moral notions *makes them* biblical."[19]

As Ramsey construes scripture, a text such as I Corinthians 13 "depicts the dispositions or virtues of Christian character that are both 'narrative dependent' and as conceptualizable as the traits of any other theory of virtues; and the love in question is steadfast covenant love firmly anchored in biblical narrative." This conceptualizing or "bracketing" of I Corinthians 13 or steadfast covenant love from its narrative context is possible and may be necessary "in order to give concentrated attention to the fruits of charity, or its formation in notions of social justice, or other 'applications'."[20] In Ramsey's many writings in applied ethics, he temporarily brackets covenant love from the narrative in order to "prolong" *agape* into public life. That he does not refer back continually to the narrative does not mean that for him *agape* is an abstract idea or general principle that is fully intelligible apart from scripture. Although rooted in biblical narrative, the principle of covenant love may be extracted from scripture and reformulated as a means of engaging in moral discourse beyond the confines of the Christian community. Thus, the Christian ethic is distinctive but not totally incomprehensible to outsiders. This approach is, in my judgment, theologically sound and more serviceable in practice than Hauerwas's alternative.

While most of my comments on the sectarian implications of Hauerwas's views will be postponed until I have discussed his social ethic, it is apparent that Hauerwas suspects that any attempt such as Ramsey's to move from the relation between biblical narrative and the formation of Christian character to decision-making and action in the realm of "quandary ethics" necessarily violates the integrity of Christian conviction narratively displayed and undermines the uniqueness of the Christian moral life.[21] This suspicion is unjustified. There is no reason in principle why one cannot do both; i.e., attend to character and to decisions or actions. The latter need not be based upon a Kantian conception of obligations binding upon all rational beings if that is the sticking point, as it seems to be for Hauerwas. It could be grounded just as easily in Christian character shaped by biblical narrative. Now, of course, Hauerwas would not allow this, and it is important to see why. Hauerwas is not simply making a formal point about the linkage between narrative and character. Rather, he has a material view of how narrative is to be understood, which he deploys in a highly normative fashion. Thus, Ramsey's reading of biblical narrative is judged inappropriate materially. While I do not share Hauerwas's judgment, there is nothing troubling about the disagreement *per se*. What is troubling is the way in which Hauerwas stipulates that a reading like Ramsey's cannot be counted formally as a reading of biblical narrative. It seems that one either understands biblical narrative as Hauerwas does or one does not understand or appreciate the role of biblical narrative at all. This conclusion cannot be sustained. To extrapolate from David Kelsey's dictum concerning the relation between exegesis and theology, it may be said that how one chooses to construe biblical narrative and which patterns are taken to be central represent "a logically prior and imaginative decision . . . which is not corrigible by the results of any kind of biblical study."[22] The construals of Ramsey and Hauerwas stand as alternative readings, but they are both readings of biblical narrative.

The last theological question to be posed here concerns Hauerwas's conception of sanctification. The cumulative effect of his accounts of virtue and character is to revive a very robust notion of sanctification in narrative dress. To what extent is it compatible with more catholic theologies' understandings of forgiveness and grace? Hauerwas clearly advises his readers to turn inward and reflect upon the coherence or incoherence of their storied lives. But self-understanding in the form of a coherent story is not the ultimate goal. Christians are to muster the imaginative and interpretive skills to construe biblical narrative correctly and then to conform themselves to its pattern. Thus, they are to live out or continue the biblical story in their own lives. This is, of course, the same mandate encountered in Frei and Barth. What is strikingly different in Hauerwas's presentation is his manifest confidence about the levels of achievement that may be expected. He seems quite sanguine about the prospect of overcoming the diffuseness, brokenness, and sin of most of our religious and moral lives. Despite his many references to the importance of the Christian community, there is relatively little emphasis placed upon the work of the Spirit or grace. Thomas Ogletree, a fellow Methodist, finds Hauerwas's account of these matters to be "incredibly intellectualistic and voluntaristic, and in Christian terms, downright Pelagian."[23]

Is this indictment fair? Consider as evidence the following from *The Peaceable Kingdom*:[24]

> Faith is not so much a combination of belief and trust, as simply fidelity to Jesus.

> Justification is only another way of talking about sanctification since it requires our transformation by initiation into the new community made possible by Jesus' death and resurrection.

Justification is but a reminder of . . . what God has done for us *by providing us with a path to follow* [emphasis added].

The Christian life is a pilgrimage of "learning to live into the story of Christ." Progress "denotes a wholeness of self that depends upon how far I have gone along that journey." To be sure, Hauerwas says we must accept our lives, God's forgiveness, the path we are to follow, and the sacraments as gifts. But there is, undeniably, a strong perfectionist current in Hauerwas's theological ethic. He strenuously denies, however, that this amounts to works righteousness.

The relation between justification and sanctification is, of course, a complex matter of both historic and ongoing significance. May or must they be seen as conceptually distinct "moments," with justification preceding sanctification? May or must they be regarded as two ways of speaking about one organic process? Hauerwas's primary concern, I suspect, is not to settle these questions in the abstract as a matter of theological method and language. Rather, he is zealous to prevent "cheap grace" and the tendency to accept justification by faith as an anthropological axiom that undercuts both the sovereignty of God's grace and the importance of imitating the life and death of Jesus of Nazareth. Thus, his position, whatever its merits may be, is consistent with his self-description as a Methodist cum high-church Mennonite.

Having noted this theological concern, I now turn to the first of the recurring philosophical issues, where further questions about Hauerwas's moral psychology will be addressed.

CHARACTER, AGENCY, AND FREEDOM

In earlier chapters, questions arose concerning the moral psychology presupposed by philosophical uses of narrative. The same kinds of questions can be put to Hauerwas. For example, in *Character and the Christian Life*, Hauerwas makes two claims regarding the connection between character and agency. These claims have been identified and analyzed by Gene Outka in the following way. First, Hauerwas says (descriptively) that the capacity to be an agent is fundamental to the concept of personhood. Second, he makes the normative claim that it is better to shape one's character than to be shaped.[25] Self-determination as such seems to be valuable in itself. Nevertheless, Outka observes that Hauerwas also makes

some strong claims for "the essential sociality of man's nature."[26] Outka
finds a "troubling unclarity" in Hauerwas's account:

> On the one side, [there is Hauerwas's] insistence that the self is
> never just the product of social forces, the distinction between
> agent and observer and the privileged position of the former, the
> gulf between what I do and what happens to me. . . . On the other,
> he appropriates as much of the Meadian legacy in social psychology
> as he can. . . . What Hauerwas neglects to ask is whether his nearly
> unqualified appropriation may not effectively jeopardize his distinc-
> tive claims about character. Even if he wishes to keep some room
> for the agent "I," it is in effect a kind of reed on the intersubjective
> field. That reed may be too slender to bear all of the presupposi-
> tions about agency which he elsewhere adopts.[27]

The "essentialist" claims for agency and sociality, in Outka's estimation,
cannot be combined in a coherent conception of character without more
explanation than Hauerwas provides.

Hauerwas acknowledges the tension and admits that he is unsure how it
might be resolved. He simply wants to emphasize character while allowing
for the social construction of the agent's perspective. Without pretending
to have solved the problem, Hauerwas suggests that his two claims might
be better formulated as: "Our agency is actually our ability to be able to
interpret and understand our dependency and through understanding
integrate our dependency into a more determinate character."[28] This claim
is reminiscent of Peter Berger's suggestion that persons are like puppets
pulled about by subtle strings according to the logic of the theater, but
who, nevertheless, may be conscious of that influence and thus be, in a
non-trivial sense, free.

As indicated earlier, Ogletree believes Hauerwas's moral psychology to
be overly "intellectualistic" and "voluntaristic." To his mind, Hauerwas
does not explore the various dynamics of sociality deeply enough. Were he
to do so, he would have to qualify his contention that character is self-
consciously formed by one's beliefs, convictions, and loyalties. These
elements would have to be seen as social constructions. Ogletree proposes
that Hauerwas be understood, not as describing the "concrete dynamics of
character formation," but rather as "explicating the nature of the normative frame of reference within which the moral quality of our lives is to be
assessed."[29] In the latter project, beliefs and convictions can be employed

legitimately to articulate materially the ways in which we believe our characters ought to be shaped. If Hauerwas were to embrace this interpretation of his work, his reply to Outka's charge of unclarity might seem more adequate.

However, the unclarity deepens when one tries to relate Hauerwas's notion of character to his understanding of vision. For Hauerwas,

> the moral life is better understood on the analogy of the aesthetic mode of seeing and beholding than in terms of action and decision. . . . The moral life does not consist just in making one right decision after another; it is the progressive attempt to widen and clarify our vision of reality.[30]

The essay from which these quotations are taken is an extended discussion of Iris Murdoch, to whom Hauerwas is, by his grateful admission, profoundly indebted. In Chapter 3 I discussed the implications of Murdoch's views for moral theory, freedom, and the possibility of moral agreement. While Murdoch is explicit about the reasons persons more often than not fail to achieve clarity of vision and the respect in which her account leaves relatively little room for freedom, Hauerwas does not attend to these implications with sufficient care. Outka is perplexed by the fact that "Hauerwas commends such an ethics of vision without asking whether this calls for any modification in his account of character, or any lessening of his own normative commitment to self-determination as such."[31] According to Outka, the radical shift to vision does both.

Hauerwas's claim that narrative is indispensable for self-understanding also raises questions in Outka's mind about the underlying moral psychology. Suppose one wished to maintain that I should struggle to evaluate critically the stories and roles bequeathed to me by my tradition. Suppose, further, that it is possible for me to apprehend two or more narratives and to ask which one I should adopt. Outka observes that both suppositions presuppose "some sense of an 'I' who stands outside any given story, who deliberates and then 'consents' to making the story his or her own." Again a question arises about "the descriptive and normative status of the 'I' which is not dissolved into the social — now narratively articulated — 'me'."[32]

Outka recognizes that Hauerwas is seeking a middle way between the extremes of the "substantialist" and "behaviorist" selves. In this, Hauerwas is following the course set by Kelsey's description of the way in which narratives can "render" agents in Barth's dogmatics.[33] Nevertheless,

Hauerwas seems to introduce claims that may well be irreconcilable. For example, Hauerwas says in one place that most of the storied convictions that "charge us morally are like the air we breathe—we never notice them."[34] Stories subject us to their particular vision of reality and cause us to make certain assumptions that are beyond conscious question or decision. Yet, in another place, Hauerwas speaks of our adopting stories or allowing them to adopt us on the basis of an evaluative process.[35] In the same essay, he reiterates a crucial claim from *Character and the Christian Life* that the "capacity to assume responsibility . . . is logically necessary if we are to claim actions as our own—and so receive praise or blame for them."[36] How these claims fit together and what status is finally assigned to the agential "I" are questions never clearly answered to Outka's satisfaction.

Outka wonders whether it is possible to distinguish between "narratives in which no provision is made for critical reflection, distancing, self-determination, etc.—narratives which, when dominant, incline always to their own perpetuation—from narratives which actually encourage self-determination." If so, are there religious or moral reasons for preferring the latter over the former? Outka also asks whether the Christian narrative may be said to actually "*require* attention to self-determination and commend a certain (suitably refined) sense of it as something valuable in itself."[37] Clearly, Outka thinks it does. Michael Goldberg makes a similar claim: "Elements of the paradigmatic Jewish story stress the importance of the capacity for self-criticism and the ability to move from blame for injustices committed in the past to moral responsibility for what shall be done in the future."[38] I think it obvious that Hauerwas would like to be able to differentiate stories in this way. Whether he could do so consistently in light of the ambiguity as to how much autonomy we have in relation to our stories is questionable.

Let us now turn to the philosophical issues that are at the heart of Hauerwas's dissatisfaction with what he calls "universal ethics" or "the standard account" (the Kantian paradigm) of moral rationality. I shall begin by reviewing an exchange of essays between Hauerwas and one of his most persistent critics, J. Wesley Robbins.

As mentioned earlier, Hauerwas frequently criticizes modern moral philosophy for failing to take into account the perspective of the moral agent and neglecting the notions of virtue and character. Robbins is one philosopher who dissents from Hauerwas's characterization of contemporary moral theory. According to Robbins, "it is simply not the case that the current view in moral philosophy has consigned agent-states to a morally subordinate role." He cites R. M. Hare and R. B. Braithwaite as two influential theorists for whom agent-states are crucially important, and he suggests that Hauerwas is really holding out for a particular kind of agent-state, "namely one's total vision of life."[39]

> To be agents at all requires a directionality that involves the development of character and virtue. Our character is the result of our sustained attention to the world which gives coherence to our intentionality. Such attention is formed and given content by the stories through which we have learned to form the story of our lives. To be moral persons is to allow stories to be told through us so that our manifold activities gain a coherence that allows us to claim them for our own.[40]

On the basis of this text, Robbins takes it to be Hauerwas's view that having such a total vision of life is the basic and necessary condition for having any morality at all and for having any specific morality (as, for example, Christian morality) in particular. To this requirement, Robbins makes three objections, which, along with Hauerwas's replies, I shall take up in turn.

First, Robbins considers Hauerwas's conception of morality as a total vision of life to be as unitary and restrictive as those theory-laden conceptions Hauerwas seeks to overturn. Such stringency is simply at odds with the fact that, in attributing moral responsibility and in assessing moral praise- and blameworthiness, we do not generally exclude persons whose lives may seem to be disorganized. "It is surely the case that there are, or at least could be, persons who either impulsively or reflectively reject just this sort of coherence as either task or accomplishment," but who nevertheless are reckoned virtuous.[41]

Hauerwas responds to this objection by denying that it is applicable. It is by no means his intention to propose yet another unitary, universal theory purporting to dictate what is to be considered 'morality'. It is precisely this sort of theorizing that he believes distorts the phenomena it attempts to explain. The expression "total vision of life" is, of course, Iris Murdoch's. Ironically, as we saw in Chapter 3, she uses it to criticize the view of R. W. Hepburn that "fables" must be highly coherent and comprehensive. When Hauerwas, following Murdoch, speaks of a vision of life, a life plan, or the story of one's life, the emphasis seems to fall on the subjectivity rather than on the scope or completeness of the vision, plan, or story. Certainly, he thinks cohesiveness and comprehensiveness are to be sought through vision and story, but he does not hold them up as necessary conditions for having morality. That Hauerwas believes them to be signs of Christian sanctification, as indicated earlier, is another matter. But Robbins's objection is wide of the mark.

Robbins's second criticism involves Hauerwas's claim that vision is uniquely suited for differentiating forms of morality. He proposes a case in which a theist and a polytheist both seek to form characters modeled after the divine love depicted in the stories of their two traditions. Further, they seem to agree on a wide range of particular moral judgments. According to Robbins: "What such an example shows is that differences in vision do not necessarily constitute moral differences. But if not, then total vision of life is not the basic determinative factor in morality after all."[42] Hauerwas dismisses this objective as an absurdity, "a studied blindness brought on by uncritical adherence to a theory."

> Of course some of the things people do in a Christian society and a polytheistic society might look the same and they might even discover areas of agreement or cooperation, but this is not a sufficient basis to claim that they share the same 'morality.' Such a claim could be sustained only if what people do is abstractly and artificially divorced from why they do what they do, i.e., what kind of agents they think themselves to be in doing what they do.[43]

Thus, Hauerwas continues to insist that agents' self-understanding is the necessary means for distinguishing one moral view from another. Again Hauerwas's claim withstands Robbins's objection.

RELATIVISM

The third and most significant charge Robbins makes against Hauerwas is that his conception of morality implies moral relativism. Once again, Robbins poses a case in which he believes Hauerwas's method breaks down. His example involves a "Mansonesque" group of killers. Captured, convicted, and imprisoned, they maintain that, although their vision of life includes a category of action called 'murder' and considers such actions to be wrong, the killings in question do not fall within that category. On the basis of their particular vision, their actions were not wrong. Regardless of the outcome of the legal proceedings, Robbins thinks that, given

Hauerwas's conception of morality, one would be "forced to admit, however reluctantly, that morally speaking, i.e., in terms of what their vision calls for of them, their actions are appropriate; they have done nothing wrong."[44] In Robbins's view, Hauerwas's only recourse would be to claim that there is an objectively correct vision for which all persons are accountable regardless of whatever particular visions they may hold, or else to admit that there are some features of morality that are vision-independent.

In his response to Robbins, Hauerwas opts for neither of the suggested replies. Instead, he observes that neither Robbins's own constructive proposal (of which I shall not speak) nor even Hare's universalizability requirement, as Hare himself has pointed out, can overcome moral fanaticism such as that in Robbins's example. Furthermore, Hauerwas does not think

> there is nor does there need to be a moral argument against the moral skeptic or relativist. Rather, . . . [he is] content to challenge the relativist or skeptic to try to live out the implications of his or her position. After all, Aristotle reminded us that practical arguments may be best in a practical discipline.[45]

Indeed, this may be the last word, but I think it is fair to say that here and elsewhere there remains a deep ambiguity in Hauerwas's position. Against Robbins's allegation, he denies that there is anything in his "analysis of the significance of vision to suggest that persons are accountable 'only for what their vision calls for of them'."[46] Yet it remains unclear, despite Hauerwas's vigorous protestations to the contrary, why this is not the case.

The problem becomes even more acute when one considers not only his remarks on vision but also his intimation that all moral schemes are utterly dependent upon narrative. I use the word "intimation" because I have not found in Hauerwas a direct statement of this claim. Nevertheless, there is sufficient evidence for thinking that he does (sometimes) hold this view. We are told, for example, that it is profoundly misleading "to try to free moral notions from their dependence on examples and narratives that display them." It is a mistake to assume "that rationality itself does not depend on a narrative." "Morally there is no neutral story. . . . Any ethical theory that is sufficiently abstract and universal to claim neutrality would not be able to form character." One cannot "conform to the moral point of view" unless one's self is formed by a narrative.[47] Equally telling is Hauerwas's favorable quotation of William Poteat's contention that moral policy statements or principles "are intelligible at all only if their implicit 'stories' are explicated. . . . The precise meaning of and hence the differences between Confucian . . . and Christian policy statements are entirely a function of their differing stories."[48] These suggestions and others like them show that Hauerwas may be attempting to have it both ways: emphasizing the agent's narrative-dependent perspective and, at the same time, continuing to insist that there is something (recognizably moral) for which all persons are accountable. Let us now explore some of Hauerwas's efforts to resolve this ambiguity.

As we have seen, Hauerwas wants to use narrative as a means of displaying the distinctiveness of the Christian life. For theologians in general, this move poses no particular problem, since in many circles natural theologies of various sorts have long been in disrepute. Thus, 'story' can be seen as simply a "new" (although it has been argued that this represents a revival of the oldest of theological methods) way of explaining the irreducible uniqueness of the Christian faith. However, for a theological *ethicist*, this approach is complicated by the fact that religious people have seldom regarded morality as their exclusive domain. Furthermore, there is the distinguished philosophical tradition that attempts to describe what 'morality' is irrespective of whatever religious or other convictions people may hold. And, of course, within Christian theology itself, there is the venerable doctrine of natural law. These three factors present a formidable obstacle for a theologian like Hauerwas who wants to speak about morality as something inextricably embedded in the distinctive perspectives of particular persons and communities. The problem is especially acute if one is concerned, as Hauerwas clearly is, to deny that his or her work entails relativism.

As critical as he is of "the ahistorical and abstract nature of modern ethical theory," Hauerwas admits "there is an aspect of our moral activity which good societies exhibit, namely, that certain things should be required of all people irrespective of why they do what they do."[49] In several writings, Hauerwas has experimented with various means of pointing to this "aspect of our morality" that is said to be universal and constant. In *Vision and Virtue*, he employs with some caution P. F. Strawson's distinction (discussed in Chapter 3) between the realms of the ethical and the moral. The ethical or higher morality refers to ideal conceptions of the good, and the lower morality encompasses universal rules or principles governing human behavior. As Strawson says, "Moral behavior is what is demanded of men as such."[50] But Hauerwas goes on to insist that this realm of lower or basic morality is not as univocal in content as the champions of such analytical tools as the principle of universalizability ‘ imagine. In fact, very little content can be specified without reference to the particularizing higher visions of the ideal.

Yet, in responding to Robbins's charge that he has simply substituted 'vision of life' for 'universalizability' in a formula as restrictive as Hare's, Hauerwas confesses that the distinction between basic and higher morality is misleading. In this context, he suggests:

> A more fruitful way of developing this point is MacIntyre's argument that all societies necessarily involve virtues like truthfulness, justice and courage. Various societies will embody or acknowledge these goods in different ways but this is only witness to their unavoidability.[51]

Once again, Hauerwas qualifies the claim by observing that "these ever present virtues are never sufficient to constitute a morality—an actual form of life that is sufficient to guide our lives and set the boundaries of moral argument."[52] Nevertheless, this approach to the problem of finding that which is universal and constant is hardly satisfactory. If virtues and vices are exhibited in narratives, and characters are formed accordingly, it would seem that the virtues embodied in various societies would be as diverse as the narratives from which they spring. So it would seem, unless it just happens to be the case that virtues are everywhere sufficiently similar that, for example, an Oxford don would have no trouble in recognizing an Australian aborigine's expression of the virtue of justice. This seems unlikely. Perhaps the Eskimo who sets his aged mother-in-law adrift on an ice floe is exercising the Eskimo virtue of compassion, but would it not be difficult for a moral theologian to recognize such an act as an example of compassion, at least in the Christian sense of that virtue? Since, in the very next paragraph, Hauerwas himself expresses the same dubiety about the possibility that both Christians and polytheists might have "respect for law" and mean the same thing by it, it is difficult to see how he intends this thesis of MacIntyre's to be understood.

In his essay "Natural Law, Tragedy and Ethics," Hauerwas makes yet another attempt to identify that which is the basis for natural morality. Criticizing the traditional theories of natural law, "understood as an independent and sufficient morality . . . [composed of the] external and minimalistic norms that Christians share with all men," Hauerwas argues that natural morality is best understood as "the cluster of roles, relations and actions the agent must order and form to have a character appropriate to the limits and possibilities of existence." What Hauerwas seems to be after is the claim that human sociability entails certain patterns of behavior that cannot be violated without risking the destruction of cooperative human life. "Natural law is therefore not based on a view of the 'nature' of man abstracted from social context, but rather, as Calvin emphasized, the natural law is but a reminder that 'to be human is to order life co-operatively.' "53 Here, Hauerwas seems to endorse the conclusion of David Little's important essay "Calvin and the Prospects for a Christian Theory of Natural Law." Unfortunately, Hauerwas does not provide as much social-scientific backing for his proposal or as many specific examples of 'moral universals' as Little does. Were he to have done so, his position would be clearer and stronger.

Elsewhere, Hauerwas even endorses the principle of universalizability (certainly a standard feature of "the standard account" defended by Hare and Marcus Singer) as "a necessary condition of morality, [though] not a sufficient condition." Acknowledging that it "expresses the fundamental commitment to regard all men as constituting a basic moral community," Hauerwas says that "it is a condition without which moral argument and judgment are not possible." Moreover, Hauerwas admits that "the principle of universalizability is a criterion of moral principles that everyone must acknowledge regardless of his status, peculiar biographical history, or the commitments and beliefs he holds."54 If this is true, surely the principle must apply regardless of one's particular narrative as well. Thus, the claim that all moral schemes are narrative-dependent would seem to be either false or, at best, an exaggeration.

We have observed Hauerwas casting about for something analogous to a theory of natural law, something ontologically weaker than traditional natural-law theory but more robust than the "thin" moral theories proffered by Rawls, Gert, and Hare. His various casual attempts to describe this vague analogue by means of the distinction between basic and higher morality, universal virtues, social requirements, and/or universalizability leave the reader confused about what exactly is being claimed. Is Hauerwas committed to the thesis that all moral schemes are narrative-dependent or is he not?

Perhaps Hauerwas is not committed to the thesis after all. Perhaps he is simply claiming that there is an important sense in which Christian morality is dependent on Christian (or biblical) narrative. In that case, he would be aligning himself with Barth and Frei along the lines I have suggested. If this is Hauerwas's intention, he ought to see that he does not need to have any stake in the universal thesis about narrative dependence. Nor does he need to hold any general anthropological thesis concerning the narrativity of human experience. He could and, I would say, should remain agnostic about both theses.

Evidence supporting this understanding of Hauerwas's project may be found in his attempt to differentiate stories on the basis of moral criteria. While as a Christian theologian Hauerwas is concerned specifically with the ways in which the stories told within the Christian community shape the lives of individual Christians, he recognizes that there are other communities and many other stories. In a pluralistic world, he thinks it important to be able to discriminate among good, less good, and evil stories. Convinced that "the test of a good story is the sort of person it shapes," Hauerwas formulates a list of "working criteria" by which stories may be evaluated:

> Any story which we adopt, or allow to adopt us, will have to display:
>
> (1) power to release us from destructive alternatives;
> (2) ways of seeing through current distortions;
> (3) room to keep us from having to resort to violence;
> (4) a sense for the tragic: how meaning transcends power.[55]

Strictly speaking, Hauerwas means to say that one should look for these effects in the lives of those shaped by a particular story. Stories whose effects meet these criteria are considered to be good.

However, it is hard to see how these criteria could provide anything resembling an "objective" evaluation of various stories. After all, in each instance, the key words ("destructive," "distortion," "violence," "tragic," and even "meaning") are narrative-dependent. Their use is not univocal. For example, a P.L.O. leader might describe a proposal for creating a Palestinian homeland as "constructive," while the prime minister of Israel might well describe it as "destructive." Nor is it likely that one could find agreement in their use of the word "violence." For one of them, it would refer to acts of terrorism, and for the other, to political decisions that are responsible for the creation of refugee camps. If a fundamental tenet of Hauerwas's program — that our use of moral concepts is, in large measure if not entirely, a function of the narratives to which we subscribe—is correct, it would seem that his criteria have no point of critical leverage outside of the evaluator's particular vision and the stories that shape it.[56]

Hauerwas himself seems to acknowledge the narrative-dependent relativity of his criteria:

> There are "criteria" of moral truthfulness though such criteria can never be independent of a substantive narrative.
>
> Morally there is no neutral story which insures the truthfulness of our particular stories.
>
> The criteria for judging among stories . . . will most probably not pass impartial inspection. For the powers of recognition cannot be divorced from one's own capacity to recognize *the good for humankind* [emphasis added].[57]

But the final phrase of the last quotation demonstrates once again the ambiguity to which I have been referring. What does Hauerwas mean by "the good for humankind"? What is the nature of our "capacity" to recognize it? Is it something to which we have access only through (and within the conceptual limitations of) our particular narratives? Is it an intuition, or is it something that is accessible through rationality itself, as the natural lawyers have always maintained?

To put the matter simply: it would seem that either the four criteria and "the good for humankind" are narrative-dependent or they are not. If they are *not* entirely narrative-dependent, then one must conclude that there is in Hauerwas's position a submerged theory of something like natural law. And if this is true, then Hauerwas ought to communicate more clearly and in more detail than he has to date what sort of a thing it is, even if this means moderating some of the claims he makes for narrative. The only viable alternative would be for Hauerwas to work within the confines of a confessional relativism and to forswear such expressions as "basic morality," "universal virtues," and "the good for humankind."

A properly circumspect and consistent reconstruction of Hauerwas's philosophical position might be stated as follows. Whatever universal, narrative-independent features of morality there may be, they ought not be assumed to generate a comprehensive account of moral rationality that would make the narrative-dependent features irrelevant, otiose, or even secondary. There is no reason in principle why philosophers may not articulate universal features of morality such as universalizability or the requisites of social existence. What they may not do, however, is assume *a priori* a substantive description of these categories. Instead they must look and see. Indeed, it is reasonable to suppose that there may be certain "family resemblances" between the moral forms of life engendered by various narratives. Nevertheless, it is unlikely that these resemblances or *de facto* overlaps would be of primary significance in the self-description of particular moralities. Nor would they play a major role in character formation or elementary moral pedagogy. In these functions, the narrative-dependent features of the morality would be the predominant influences. In fact, they would be indispensable. Important aspects of morality would be epistemologically dependent upon narrative.[58] Of course, these claims are more modest than some of those actually made in Hauerwas's writings. Were they to represent his (re-)considered judgments, extensive revisions of his earlier work would be necessary.

What might prevent Hauerwas *qua* Christian theologian from limiting himself to offering an internal description of the Christian moral life under the cultural-linguistic model of religion? Perhaps he would be reluctant to adopt a stance of "soft perspectivism" or confessional relativism. In discussing Frei's observation that realistic biblical narrative may be considered "history-like," Hauerwas worries that Frei's proposal may be soft on the question of historical truth: "It would be disastrous if this emphasis on the significance of story for theological reflection became a way to avoid the question of how religious convictions or stories may be true or false, i.e., you have your story and we have ours and there is no way to judge the truth of either."[59] Indeed, it would be disastrous. However, as I argued in Chapter 5, the cultural-linguistic model is hospitable to truth claims. In fact, it can accommodate truth claims more readily than the experiential-expressive model. Under the latter, one would have to maintain, to use Hauerwas's criteria, that the Christian narrative is the most evocative of "release from destructive alternatives," alternatives to violence, and a "sense for the tragic." Since there can be no logically intrinsic upper limit on degrees of evocation, it would be impossible to assign any meaning to the claim that the Christian narrative is unsurpassably true in these respects. Concern for the possibility of making truth claims should not bar Hauerwas from a more straightforward and consistent appropriation of the cultural-linguistic model.

By his own admission, there is no "story of stories" and no story-neutral, objective access to the way things really are. "All we can do," he says, "is

compare stories to see what they ask of us and the world we inhabit."
Hauerwas avers that he has no wish "to claim that the stories which
Christians and Jews identify are the only stories that offer skills for truthfulness in the moral life."[60] There is no reason why he should not regard
non-Judeo-Christian narratives and the characters they evoke as authentic,
morally worthy forms of life. Not to be able to demonstrate objectively
that Christian narrative actually corresponds to ultimate reality is no
disgrace. But to employ vision, character, and story in a self-description of
the Christian moral life within the community and its narrative may be
the most truthful tack Hauerwas can take.[61]

THE CHURCH'S SOCIAL-ETHICAL TASK

Now that Hauerwas's program for theological ethics has been explored
and the recurrent philosophical issues have been analyzed, I want to
examine his understanding of social ethics. Hauerwas's account of the
social-ethical task of the church reflects a narrowing of focus on the
self-description of the Christian community. However, I find his normative conception of the church's task inadequate.

In the essays that make up A Community of Character: Toward a Constructive Christian Social Ethic, Hauerwas aspires to write as one who
occupies the office of theologian in the church. Acknowledging that his
thought is neither disciplined nor constrained by the realities and ambiguities
of any concrete church, he says that he thinks and writes "not only for the
church that does exist but for the church that should exist if we were more
courageous and faithful."[62] This freedom from any particular confession or
institution allows Hauerwas to follow his own theological tastes as he
designs a social ethic fit for a church of his own imagining. While "visionary"
reflection is not to be despised or depreciated, it is one of the principal
sources of my discomfort with Hauerwas's constructive Christian social
ethic. A number of my disagreements with Hauerwas, to be identified
below, stem from the extreme ideality of his conception of the church and
its ministry to the world.

Hauerwas states that his intention is "to reassert the social significance of
the church as a distinct society with an integrity peculiar to itself." 'Integrity'
refers, not only to the church's particularity as a cultural-linguistic community, but also to the uniqueness of its social ethic. The most important
social task of Christians, according to Hauerwas, "is nothing less than to be

a community capable of hearing the story of God we find in scripture and living in a manner faithful to that story." Specifically, this means that "the primary social task of the church is to be itself—that is, a people who have been formed by a story that provides them with the skills for negotiating the danger of this existence, trusting in God's promise of redemption." The distinctiveness of the Christian community is a function of its story. "The form and substance of a community is narrative dependent and therefore what counts as 'social ethics' is a correlative of the content of that narrative."[63]

Neglect of the Christian community's narrative dependence, in Hauerwas's opinion, has led to the erroneous presumption that Christian social ethics is primarily a matter of "securing more equitable forms of justice," developing "social theories or strategies to make America work," and transforming our "basic social and economic structures in order to aid individuals in need."[64] Moreover, it has been assumed, falsely according to Hauerwas, that secular political involvement by the church is the best way to achieve these goals. To him, all of this seems very mistaken. Christians ought not "assume that [their] task as Christians is to make history come out right."[65] Politics ought not be associated primarily with social change. "Rather the 'political' question crucial to the church is what kind of community the church must be to be faithful to the narratives central to Christian convictions."[66] For Hauerwas, the internal ordering of the Christian community is the foremost political concern. Social ethics, therefore, is the interpretive and descriptive task of articulating the virtues and characters appropriate to the Christian story and conducive to living morally in the world as it is.

While this may seem to be a rather conservative program, it is evident that Hauerwas, like most sectarians, is highly critical of contemporary American society. One of his principal objectives is to "challenge the dominant assumption of contemporary Christian social ethics that there is a special relation between Christianity and some form of liberal democratic social system."[67] Indeed, he rejects the notion that the church should provide an ethos for any form of social or political organization. Instead, the church must "provide the space and time necessary for developing skills of interpretation and discrimination sufficient to help us recognize the possibilities and limits of our society." As a community shaped by the authoritative Christian narrative, the church should be the "primary polity" through which Christians "gain the experience to negotiate and make positive contributions to whatever society in which [they] may find [themselves]." In this way, the church stands as "a 'contrast model' for all polities that know not God" and "as an international society . . . ; a sign that God, not nations, rule [sic] this world." To shirk these responsibilities would be to defect to that "most convenient" of idolatries, "the presumed primacy of the nation state."[68]

For the church to foster interpretive and discriminative skills, it must be what James Gustafson calls "a community of moral discourse." Only through discussion, recognizing and listening to the other, does the Christian community "find the way of obedience."[69]

> There is no inherent reason that Christians must agree about every issue. . . . What is required is not that Christians agree, but that their agreements and their disagreements reflect their theological convictions. The church no less than any community must provide the political process through which moral issues can be disposed and adjudicated. What is unique about the church is not that such a process is required, or that it does not always produce agreement; what is unique is the kind of concerns that are made subject to the process, the theological convictions that shape our reasoning, and the way the discussion is governed by love.[70]

Nevertheless, Hauerwas is not prepared to jettison the notion of authority. Not everyone's opinion is to be counted equally. The theologian *qua* social ethicist contributes to the discussion by interpreting the authoritative narratives and articulating the appropriate convictions and characters. Thus, the church may function as "a school for virtue."[71]

In the North American political context, the targets of the church's critique are the moral assumptions of political liberalism. The fundamental problem with liberalism, in Hauerwas's estimation, is that it is based upon a narrative—here he refers to it as a "myth"—that holds that no shared history, tradition, or narrative is necessary for societal cooperation and cohesion:

> A people do not need a shared history; all they need is a system of rules that will constitute procedures for resolving disputes as they pursue their various interests. Thus liberalism is a political philosophy committed to the proposition that a social order and corresponding mode of government can be formed on self-interest and consent.[72]

Liberalism's pernicious moral assumptions include the notions that the individual is the sole source of authority, that civic duty and public interest are unspecifiable, that public policy should seek to maximize the aggregate of self-interests, that all human relationships should take so far as may be possible the form of market exchange, and, thus, that the essence of rational purpose is the pursuit of possessions.[73]

Although Hauerwas acknowledges that the fruits of political liberalism are by no means all bad, and that in a sense "we are all liberals," Christians must submit liberalism's moral assumptions to radical critique.[74] This critical questioning cannot be a matter of simply "qualifying some of the excess of liberalism" or proposing ways of fine-tuning the mechanisms of the liberal state for a more equitable distribution of goods. Too often, in Hauerwas's opinion, the church has succumbed to this temptation and therefore has been derelict in its duty. Because Christians already have a primary, authoritative story, they may not acquiesce to the story of liberalism, which entices them "to believe that freedom and rationality are independent of narrative—i.e., we are free to the extent we have no story." By presenting a "contrast model" or "alternative polity," the church is able to "chart forms of life for the development of virtue and character as public concerns."[75] Hauerwas considers this to be a genuine and indispensable contribution to the social order because

> the problem in liberal societies is that there seems to be no way to encourage the development of public virtue without accepting a totalitarian strategy from the left or an elitist strategy from the right. By standing as an alternative to each, the church may well help free our social imagination from those destructive choices.[76]

Since the critical tools for such an emancipation cannot be found within the liberal tradition, it is imperative that Christians not be reticent in using the language and interpretive skills of their tradition and its narrative to envision new possibilities, what Hauerwas calls "a politics of trust." It should be noted, however, that faithfulness to God and his story requires this critique. Its possible benefit to society-at-large is, for Hauerwas, a secondary consideration.

The perspectives on the church and social ethics sketched above demonstrate that Hauerwas's views may be described in fairness as sectarian. His appreciative essay on the theological ethics of John Howard Yoder and his "ecclesial preference to be a high-church Mennonite" corroborate this judgment.[77] Nonetheless, Hauerwas insists that this description is inappropriate. He denies, frequently and quite strenuously, any suggestion that his social ethic involves or justifies "a rejection of the world or a withdrawal from the world."[78] From his claim that "the first social task of the church is to be the church," Hauerwas draws a corollary, that "the church must serve the world on its own terms."[79] That the world may regard the church's faithful service as disloyalty does not perturb Hauerwas. Service there must be, but it must be performed in a way that does not compromise the church's integrity. As in the case of the Christian critique of liberalism, the form of the church's service may be nothing more than an ordering of its own community so as to display an alternative polity and character formation. To be sure, Hauerwas would object to the diminutive "nothing more than" since, as we have seen, he considers such a stance to be a valuable witness—more valuable than many ecclesiastical actions and pronouncements directed to the outside world. If his views are at odds with widely held conceptions of the church's social ethics, Hauerwas believes the latter must give way.

Thomas Ogletree observes that Hauerwas advocates a sectarian witness "without at the same time attending to the social conditions necessary to give authenticity to that witness."[80]

> As long as Christian people are heavily involved in the major institutions of a society and are dependent in fundamental ways for their well-being on those institutions, they are not likely to have the personal and social resources necessary for sustaining a radical witness to society. A call for a sectarian witness which does not from the beginning address these problems is itself apt to be a temptation to self-deception, i.e., a justification for noninvolvement with persons and groups struggling for justice. . . . [81]

If Christians are to avoid being in "bad faith," they may have to alter their social conditions. There is some evidence to suggest that Hauerwas may be willing to take the necessary steps. For example, he stipulates that "Christian social ethics can only be done from the perspective of those who do not seek to control national or world history but who are content to live 'out of control'."[82] But whether this perspective may be adopted empathetically from within institutions or whether it requires morally conscientious Christians to remove themselves from institutions and to divest themselves of power, Hauerwas does not say. While Ogletree's caveat was issued before the publication of Hauerwas's most recent reflection on social ethics, I see no reason for its rescission.

In any event, Hauerwas clearly wishes to move in a sectarian direction even if he doesn't want it described that way and even if he may not yet be ready to accept all of the attendant implications. In terms of H. Richard Niebuhr's classic typology, it might be said that, in rejecting the "Christ of Culture" type and resisting the "Christ transforming Culture" type, Hauerwas has ended up with those who hold the "Christ against Culture" position. This location within the typology would not discomfort Hauerwas. In his opinion, the popularity of the "transformation" image and the strategy of involvement it is usually understood to entail are the result of

> a failure to discriminate between different kinds of cultures and different aspects of any culture for what might be transformed and what might be accepted. Niebuhr's uncritical use of the word 'culture' allowed him to load the case too simply against the "Christ against Culture" type and to present the "Christ transforming Culture" type in a far too uncritical light.[83]

Moreover, Hauerwas suspects that, to the extent the transformist position succeeds in its mission, it tends to become yet another version of "Christ of Culture." Hauerwas's criticisms of "transformation" and Niebuhr's depiction of it are not without merit, and he is certainly correct in saying that Niebuhr's "account of types is not a sufficient argument for [or against] a particular social ethic."[84] Therefore, I shall indicate briefly the reasons why I consider Hauerwas's position to be inadequate.

Hauerwas's admission that he writes for and about a church that *ought* to exist is telling. Earlier I introduced some objections to his conception of sanctification, one of which was that he assumes too much about our ability to conform ourselves to the Christian story. Here it appears that substantial conformity to the example of Jesus is a requirement for membership in church. Hauerwas calls upon members of the Christian community "to be like God: perfect as God is perfect," and "to be like Jesus."[85] Certainly, this is a rigorous standard, and, in the context of Hauerwas's view of justification-sanctification, it becomes a "new law," a harsh legalism. Were Hauerwas to follow the implications of his position to the logical conclusion identified by Ogletree, his would be a church composed exclusively of those who have successfully disassociated themselves from all the other (non-Christian) stories of which they were a part and from the secular "offices" they previously held.

Still, it would be unfair to say that Hauerwas does not attend to the idea of Christian vocation in society. He wants Christians to criticize, to offer alternative models, and, most important, to be the church. The last surely involves a tangible contribution to social welfare, but since it must be carried out on (Hauerwas's idea of) the church's terms, the result is a narrow conception of Christian vocation.

Recalling his stipulations that Christians must "live out of control," that they must not "try to make history come out right," and that "Christian social ethics is not best written from the perspective of the Secretary of State," one supposes that Hauerwas would want to qualify the fairly common notion that Christians may and should serve their neighbors by employing whatever talents and resources may be at their disposal for the upbuilding of the wider community.[86] Reading Hauerwas, one is prompted to wonder, in the spirit of Luther's famous essay, whether not only soldiers but also judges, legislators, union officials, corporate executives, or even plumbers, too, may be saved.

The soteriological question aside—I don't think Hauerwas ever presumes to answer it—it is clear that for Hauerwas faithfulness to Jesus requires Christians to forswear violence and coercion. Indeed, Christian pacifism has emerged as a major theme in his most recent writings. Can Christians in good conscience participate in institutions (e.g., the criminal justice system, the military, the United States Congress, or the African National Congress) that involve coercion and sometimes violence? Can they work for companies that produce the instruments of coercion?

Hauerwas is extremely reluctant to pronounce a ban on particular occupations or involvements: "I have no interest in legitimating and/or recommending a withdrawal of Christians or the church from social or political affairs. I simply want them there as Christians and as church."[87] Of course, being there (in General Dynamics or in the United States Navy) "as Christians" is entailed in what I referred to as the common notion of Christian vocation in society. Christians in all walks of life are obligated to ask themselves whether their occupations contribute to the well-being of their neighbors. If Hauerwas requires more than this conscientious self-examination—as it seems he does—then he should explain more clearly than he has to date exactly which kinds and levels of involvement in coercive, potentially violent institutions are acceptable and which are not.

Hauerwas says, however, that this "can not be determined in principle but depends upon the individual character and nature of individual societies and their governments." He is prepared to grant that "it may be possible . . . for a Christian in some societies to be a policeman, a prison warden etc."[88] Which societies these might be, he does not say. His hesitancy may reflect his aversion for rules and his methodological allegiance to virtue and character. But this suggests that his method may be inadequate for social ethics. When the Christian community hears one of its moral theologians confess that he is a pacifist and argue that all Christians ought to be pacifists, the sisters and brothers may well wonder what specifically is required of them in their callings. That, it seems to me, is *part* of what Christian social ethics is about. If an ethics of virtue and character shaped by narrative does not yield more determinate conclusions, its utility is doubtful.[89]

Similarly, there is little attention paid to senses in which the church *qua* institution is a church in society. When Hauerwas speaks of the church conforming its own life to the story of God, it is not clear that he understands that to include the church's institutional roles as employer, owner of property, purchaser of goods and services, and administrator of educational and social-service institutions. Hauerwas's church, as both the people of God in the world and as an institution in society, is an abstract idealization. While I have no wish to deny that Hauerwas's envisioning of the church as it might be may contribute to both the church as it is and to society, in my judgment that contribution is a limited one.

Both sociologically and theologically, the Christian church is a church *in* society. Christians, therefore, have a responsibility to extend or "prolong" the norm of neighbor-love into public life. Christian social ethics must be concerned about the ethos, habits, practices, and policies of society. This concern is expressed in addressing social practice in intelligible and constructive ways. That is not to say that the address must never be critical. Hauerwas is quite right to insist that sometimes a radical critique is in order. Where there is deep disagreement, it is neither honest nor helpful to pretend otherwise. However, disagreements may be explored, assumptions challenged, and alternatives proposed. The church has a theological stake, in faithfulness to God and his purposes for creation, in keeping the conversation going so far as may be possible.

In the third and again in the present chapter, I have expressed a preference for narratives and communities that seek such opportunities for conversation and celebrate whatever agreements or "overlaps" may be discovered. It seems to me that Christian social ethics should be eager to exploit those *de facto* overlaps for the good of society as a whole. Thus, I am distressed by the degree to which Hauerwas revels in differences and disagreements.[90] He is largely indifferent or, at best, insufficiently committed to dialogue beyond the parameters of Christian narrative and the community it shapes. His disposition in this regard is not only a consequence of his sectarian understanding of the church's social task and ethics but of his nearly exclusive focus on virtue and character as well. His distaste for principles, rules, and decisions has odd consequences. For example, Hauerwas makes much of the narratively mandated Christian virtue of hospitality. Christians must be "ready to offer hospitality to the stranger."[91] Although it is not an issue he discusses, it seems reasonable to suppose that Christians whose characters are formed by the Christian narrative might be active in the "sanctuary movement," assisting (even to the point of civil disobedience) aliens who enter the United States illegally in search of immigration status as political refugees. But were these hospitable Christians to share Hauerwas's view of Christian social ethics, they would have little or nothing to say about what United States immigration policy ought to be. If Hauerwas were to be consistent, he would relinquish the possibility of advising (however generally) on matters of public policy. As a theologian, an interpreter of the Christian narrative, he simply would have nothing of relevance to contribute.

Fairness requires me to observe that on occasion Hauerwas seems to recognize the need for public moral discourse. For instance, he is willing to grant that the "standard account" of moral theory

> embodies concerns which any substantive moral narrative must respect: a high regard for public discourse, the demand that we be able to offer reasons for acting at once cogent and appropriate, and a way to develop critical skills of discrimination and judgment. Finally, any morality depends on a capacity to generate and articulate moral principles that can set boundaries for proper behavior and guide our conduct.[92]

By implication, this would seem to apply to Christian narrative and morality.

Elsewhere he maintains that, in his Christian social ethics, "it is not [his] intention to deny the importance of such issues" as "policies and strategies to insure just distribution of resources or the theories of justice presupposed by such policies."[93] This language seems to leave open the possibility that issues such as these might be treated—as important if not fundamental questions of Christian social ethics—in such a way that the particularity and integrity of the church would not be denied or compromised. Indeed, Hauerwas now speaks of Christians having a duty to participate in public-policy debates. He, himself, has addressed government ethics committees concerning experimentation on children and *in vitro* fertilization.[94] In my judgment, public moral discourse is both possible and necessary. That Hauerwas contributes to it is all to the good. But how it coheres with the predominant direction of his narrative program and whether his method is well suited for such discussion remain unclear.

CONCLUSION

In sum, Hauerwas's work is an important contribution to contemporary theological ethics. He has rehabilitated the long-neglected notions of virtue and character. By rooting his ethic in the Christian community and its narrative, he has redirected attention toward scripture and the distinctive features of the Christian moral life. That the meanings of and relations between the emphases are, as I have demonstrated, unclear and sometimes problematic does not void the significance of his project. The ambiguities may be attributable to the fact that his favorite genre is the occasional essay. Although he often takes note of criticisms, his replies are frequently sketchy and fail to indicate what adjustments he is prepared to make. His perspective is always provocative and usually insightful. It deserves a more deliberate and detailed statement. Far from denying the usefulness of narrative for Christian ethics, my questions and criticisms are intended to suggest an agenda for further reflection. Undoubtedly, Hauerwas's work will continue to endow that enterprise.

8

A CONCLUDING ASSESSMENT

It is time to draw together the results of my theological inquiry into the relation between narrative and morality. What are we to make of so many and such diverse appeals to narrative? 'Narrative' is, certainly, in vogue. Is it merely an academic "buzzword" or a fashionable rhetorical umbrella under which all sorts of related and unrelated ideas seek shelter? Unsatisfying as it may seem to narrative's fans and critics alike, my answer is "yes and no." Yes, narrative is often used quite vaguely and uncritically. It was possible to be a critic of Kant, a relativist, a historicist, an antifoundationalist, an aficionado of cultural diversity, a 'realistic' reader of the Bible, a 'dogmatic' theologian, or just a lover of stories long before philosophers and religionists began talking narrative. But, no, narrative in some of its manifestations, anyway, should not be dismissed as a passing fad.

As I have attempted to demonstrate in Chapters 2, 3, and 4, narrative is ingredient to the historical understanding of ourselves and our communities. MacIntyre's narrative understanding of moral traditions and theories (e.g., his account of emotivism) is illuminating. The meaning of moral practices and the use of moral concepts can be elucidated in terms of their place within narratives. However, it is wrong to suggest that we are, of necessity, prisoners of our stories. We can gain critical distance from the narratives that have influenced us and thereby exert a certain freedom over against them.

Moreover, there are features of morality that are not dependent upon narrative. Some account of basic moral rules or social requirements is defensible philosophically without appeal to narrative. Such accounts of common morality can stand apart from and be used to evaluate (morally) particular narratives. Of course, some narratives may recognize or endorse these universal features, and those that do are morally preferable to those that do not.

An adequate philosophical account of morality as a social institution must admit the necessity of rules, as both MacIntyre and Murdoch acknowledge. I have shown that the two-tiered accounts of morality offered by Gert and Strawson are not incompatible with some of the claims made for narrative. Moral rules required for social existence and narratives displaying moral virtues and ideals are jointly ingredient to a coherent and plausible understanding of morality.

In my examination of the theological literature in Chapter 5, I found that the introduction of the category narrative redirects attention toward the church and its scripture. For this reason, narrative is a welcome feature of current methodological discussion. Construing the Bible as narrative can facilitate the theological appropriation of scripture. Furthermore, it is a use of scripture that is less arcane and more accessible to laypersons than some widely practiced alternatives. Continuity between second-order theological discourse and the liturgy and popular piety of the church is a beneficial by-product of reading biblical texts or the Bible as a whole as narrative.

The postliberal-particularistic reading of biblical narrative described by Frei is by far the most promising approach to "narrative theology." When theology is considered the self-description of the Christian cultural-linguistic community, narrative provides conceptual tools for displaying distinctive features of scripture and the Christian tradition. Biblical narrative is seen to depict a world that is at once the world of the story and the world of our everyday existence. As the Christian community's self-description, theology is, in Frei's terms, the "conceptual redescription" of the world of biblical narrative in belief and life.

Nevertheless, as I have suggested, narrative is not a universal solvent for all theological problems or disagreements. Biblical narrative can be construed in different ways and used to warrant a variety of theological proposals. For example, in Chapter 6 I argued that construing scripture as narrative does not resolve the issues concerning the use of scripture in ethics. Scripture, even when it is conceived as narrative, can be employed in an irreducibly "great variety" (Gustafson) of ways. Perhaps the strongest claim that can be made in this regard for a narrative construal of scripture is that it contributes to the proper understanding of some of the explicitly moral teachings of the Bible.

A TEST CASE

Just how useful is narrative in theological ethics? I now turn to a concrete test case. Does attention to biblical or Christian narrative specify how Christians ought to understand a particular set of issues pertaining to marriage and the family? Let us see how Hauerwas's social ethic explicates these aspects of the Christian moral life. It may be useful to begin with a brief sketch of the popular view of marriage and family against which a Christian narrative perspective sets its face. According to Hauerwas, the narrative of liberal society has promulgated the notion that the family is nothing more than a contractual society. Marriage and family provide the context for more intimate and satisfying interpersonal relationships than are available elsewhere. By specializing in emotions, the family offers a refuge from the rigors of industrial society and the exigencies of the market. Mobility and the quest for freedom and privacy break traditional bonds of kinship, and the nuclear family emerges as the largest sustainable social unit. But even here the ties are not particularly strong. As evidence, Hauerwas cites the facts that children are regarded as having "rights" over against their parents and that husbands are without rights if their wives wish to have an abortion. In *Planned Parenthood v. Danforth,* the United States Supreme Court held "abortion [to be] a purely personal right of the woman, and the status of marriage can place no limitation on personal rights."[1] Spouses and children remain atomistic. Their relationships are not much different from those between especially friendly strangers. Thus, in liberal society, the traditional family seems a morally irrational anomaly.

From the perspective of Hauerwas's Christian social ethic, things look very different. Marriage is seen, not as a private contractual arrangement for the emotional fulfillment of the parties, but rather as an embodiment of moral and social purposes within the wider community. "Unless marriage has a purpose beyond being together it will certainly be a hell." For Hauerwas, the *telos* of marriage is the family. As an "intergenerational" institution (rather than as an interpersonal association between atomistic individuals), the family "is morally crucial for our existence as the only means we have of binding time." It provides "a story of and for the self" that preserves and passes on a moral tradition. As a Christian institution, marriage is "political" in that "it requires a community that has a clear sense of itself and its mission and the place of the family within that mission." The community is, of course, the church formed by the Christian story. Thus, the Christian ethic of marriage and family (and sexuality in general) is not Constantinian, but only for those "who share the purposes of the community gathered by God."[2]

"Integral to the Christian understanding of the political significance of marriage" is the claim that the unitive and procreative ends of marriage are connected. Hauerwas believes that for this connection to be intelligible an account is needed of why marriage should be considered exclusive. His explanation is twofold. First, "Christians have legitimated such commitments because they believe the 'good' that constitutes the church is served only by our learning to love and serve our neighbors as we find them in our mates and children."[3] Concern for the particular attachments required by the community is seen as overriding any general welfare considerations. The second explanation is that loyalty to God and his story necessitates our fidelity. "Our commitment to exclusive relations witnesses to God's pledge to his people, Israel and the church, that through his exclusive commitment to them, all people will be brought into his Kingdom."[4] Faithfulness in marriage is, thus, an antitype of biblical narrative. "Fidelity makes sense only if it occurs in a community that has a mission in which marriage serves a central political purpose."[5]

Supposing the stipulated prerequisites are met, how does Hauerwas explain the link between unitive and procreative ends? Explicitly rejecting appeals to biological nature or natural law, Hauerwas looks to the self-understanding of the early Christian community. The early church undermined assumptions about the naturalness of marriage and family by legitimating singleness "as a form of life symbolizing the necessity of the church to grow through witness and conversion." By giving up heirs, single Christians living "between the times" manifested their confidence in the coming Kingdom. At the same time, the early church also sponsored marriage and procreation as "the symbol of the church's understanding that the struggle will be long and hard."[6] Both were regarded as equally valid modes of life.[7]

Hauerwas believes that Christians today have children for similar reasons. Christians of all centuries procreate within the same narrative context. Through biblical narrative and the story of the church, Christians regard children as "a sign of their hope, in spite of the considerable evidence to the contrary, that God has not abandoned this world."[8] Confidence in God's trustworthiness allows Christians sufficient confidence in themselves to bring new life into the world. Hauerwas says there is a "joyful," "Christian duty" to receive and welcome children, "not as something that is 'ours,' but as a gift which comes from another."[9] He even goes so far as to suggest that "the refusal to have children can be an act of ultimate despair that masks the deepest kind of self-hate and disgust"—the fear that one's story is not worthwhile enough to pass on. For Christians, voluntary childlessness also involves defection from the community's mission to participate in God's continuing creation: "For children are our anchors in history, our pledge and witness that the Lord we serve is the Lord not only of our community, but of all history. The family is, therefore, symbolically central for the meaning of the existence of the Christian people."[10] This is the larger purpose to which marriage points. Marriage "is a heroic task that can be accomplished only by people who have developed the [necessary] virtues and character" correlative to the appropriation of Christian narrative.

The account of marriage and family sketched above is a concatenation of themes: divine providence, self-esteem, the church as a moral community, and the church's historic mission in service to God's coming Kingdom. At every juncture the linkage is said to be warranted by Christian narrative. Nevertheless, Hauerwas makes a number of highly controverted claims. If one is to disagree with Hauerwas, is it necessary to argue without reference to narrative (say, in terms of nature, reason, or natural law), or may one simply construe the biblical narrative differently? I shall demonstrate that the latter is the case.

Witness to the Kingdom is not the only biblically narrated and theologically narratable theme in regard to marriage. Paul Ramsey's perspective (which Hauerwas finds "arbitrary," "authoritarian," and "unintelligible") offers an alternative reading of biblical narrative. Ramsey derives the norm of marital fidelity from the "one-flesh" unity displayed in the Genesis narrative. The contextual backing for this reading is, according to Ramsey,

> the narratable notion of covenant love in search of an understanding of embodiment. It [is] Karl Barth's relational *imago Dei,* and the understanding of man-womanhood in his doctrine of creation. [It is] a modest explication of Barth's famous double movement: "Creation as the External Basis of the Covenant" and "The Covenant as the Internal Basis of Creation."[11]

Earlier I noted that Ramsey faults Hauerwas for his general inattention to the status of covenant love. Here, the inattention takes Hauerwas far afield from the doctrine of creation. Ramsey describes Hauerwas's attempt to ground fidelity in the church's commitment to exclusive relationships and mission in history as "an assortment of current anthropological soteriological insights diligently in search of an account of biblical narrative that fits."[12]

Karl Barth's credentials as a theologian of biblical narrative are certainly beyond question. It is instructive to observe that Barth regards marriage as a divine vocation or office in the community that has an inherent meaning and integrity of its own:

> Marriage is not subordinate to the family, but the family (the relationship between parents and children which is itself an independent form) to marriage. Marriage as a life-partnership implies, of course, an inner readiness for children and therefore for the family.... It is in no way conditioned by the coexistence of children.... [W]hen we remember that the question of posterity has lost its decisive significance in the time of the new covenant, we surely cannot fail to recognize that husband and wife form a sphere of fellowship independent of child or family.[13]

Barth's reference to the "new covenant" includes the idea that "*the Child has been born.*" By placing himself with the earliest Christians "between the times," Hauerwas neglects not only the doctrine of creation but also, in Ramsey's words, "the Alpha who is within yet before . . . [and] the Omega beyond yet within the narrative." Hauerwas's perspective on marriage and family is too "narrowly temporal. . . . [His world is] too flat to be a faithful account of the world created by biblical narrative."[14]

Within the Christian tradition, marriage has been understood in a variety of ways: ontologically, as a sacramental union reflecting the bond between Christ and the church; teleologically, as an order of creation for the procreation of the people of God; and relationally, as a society ordained by God to rescue men and women from primordial loneliness. The last understanding received special emphasis among seventeenth-century English Puritans. Their conception of marriage was no less rooted in biblical narrative than is Hauerwas's. For example, John Milton understood the first two chapters of Genesis, and especially Genesis 2:18, to depict the relationship of Adam and Eve as an archetypal remedy for loneliness:

"From which words so plain lesse cannot be concluded, . . . then that in God's intention a meet and happy conversation is the chiefest and noblest end of marriage."[15] Certainly, this is very different from Hauerwas's contention that marriage without some further purpose beyond companionship or mutual fulfillment is "hell."

My point has been to illustrate that narrative is not a universal solvent for any and every disagreement in theological ethics. The distinctive and disputed features of Hauerwas's ethics are not the consequence of attending to biblical or Christian narrative. Rather, they are the precipitate of his idiosyncratic interpretation of the narrative. In other words, Hauerwas makes substantive theological judgments for which he provides narrative warrants. Others read the narrative differently and, accordingly, make different judgments. While the plurality of readings is not infinite — at least where the church and a confessional interpretive tradition are accorded authority — it is ineradicable. Thus, narrative cannot be expected to overcome the diversity of judgments in theological ethics. Perhaps Hauerwas would concur, but there is in his writings a disturbing tendency to dismiss differing opinions as being insufficiently grounded in Christian narrative, when, in fact, they may simply be grounded in alternative readings. This seems to be the case in the disagreements between Hauerwas, Ramsey, and Barth on marriage and procreation. When the distinction between reading and readings is overlooked, theological argument cannot be incisive.

NARRATIVE AND THE CHURCH IN SOCIETY

Theological ethics, as I understand it, is the explication of the Christian moral life in two modes: Christian righteousness and civic (or secular) righteousness. In the case of the former, narrative plays the indispensable role Hauerwas describes. By displaying dispositions and virtues that shape character and "master images," "types" or "analogies" that conduce to self-understanding and conduct appropriate to the Christian life of neighbor-love, narrative depicts the fruits of faith in God's gracious love for sinners. In the latter case, the Christian moral life as civic righteousness, narrative is less serviceable. When one's task is to show how Christian love is elaborated in diverse vocations and offices in society, one must have recourse to principles, rules, and reason. To be sure, some of the rules — for example, the Ten Commandments — may be biblical or even biblically narrated. Yet narrative per se as a depiction of virtue and character does not suffice for an account of the work of Christian love toward greater approximations of justice in the world that God has made. As foci in theological ethics, narrative, vision, virtue, and character are necessary. But they are not sufficient.

In the twenty-ninth chapter of the Book of Jeremiah, it is narrated that the prophet wrote to the exiles in Babylon: "Thus says the Lord of hosts, the God of Israel. . . . Seek the welfare of the city where I have sent you into exile, and pray to the Lord on its behalf, for in its welfare you will find your welfare." If Christians today are to "seek the good of the city" in the civil community, they must recognize that their neighbors are informed by radically different and diverse stories. Social cooperation requires at least a modicum of common language or a conceptual framework in which disputes, problems, and solutions may be discussed.[16] An exclusive concentration on Christian narrative will not generate the resources for such conversation.

Furthermore, the sorts of issues and problems Christians confront in the civil community are rarely, if ever, resolved conclusively by means of the direct application of narrative. For example, biblical narrative may provide a mandate for the feeding of the poor, but it contributes little to the discussion of how it should be accomplished. Should the poor be fed by means of privately operated soup kitchens, public assistance, food stamps, distribution of government surpluses, or a negative income tax (a guaranteed annual income)? Which of these approaches best approximate justice? What roles should efficiency and cost play in such a policy decision? These and similar questions in social ethics are not answerable simply by appeals to biblical narrative.

Theological ethics cannot afford to limit itself to the explication of biblical narrative. In the preceding chapter, I indicated that Hauerwas, for all his attention to narrative, has some regard for public moral discourse and the need to give reasons for our moral decisions and actions. Moreover, I described his search for something analogous to natural law that would make possible the moral evaluation of narratives. A good candidate for that analogue is an account of the moral rules prerequisite to social cooperation and moral discourse in a pluralistic society. Such a narrative-independent account of common morality is more modest than that furnished by traditional (ontological) natural-law theory. Nevertheless, it supplies a 'natural' basis for perduring universal moral norms. As long as such a description of the narrative-independent features of morality does not purport to be comprehensive, thereby obviating attention to narrative-dependent features, there is no good reason for Hauerwas's continued resistance to a bi-level theory of morality.

While the moral rules may not encompass as much of morality as some philosophers are prone to imagine, they engage more of it than many proponents of narrative are willing to admit. The conclusion of my inquiry is that narrative is necessary but insufficient for Christian ethics. To describe the moral realm as an interweaving of narrative-dependent and narrative-independent features does not nullify the distinctive contribution of narrative to the texture of the Christian moral life.

AN AGENDA FOR FUTURE WORK

In conclusion I offer some suggestions for future discussion of narrative and morality. As I read the existing literature, more questions have been raised than have been answered. This means, of course, that the conversation is likely to continue. Here are some points at which further reflection is needed.

First, let no one employ the term "narrative" without carefully spelling out what it refers to and how it is to be used. If narrative is used to refer to "the Christian story" or "the Christian tradition," its use is obfuscating. If it is used to refer to the way in which cultures shape characters, then it seems too narrow. As Wayne Meeks observes, "the moral formation of a community surely requires other means besides telling stories: for example, ritual and liturgy, which do have narrative components, but which cannot simply be subsumed under that category." If narrative is used as a shorthand reference for the manifold ways cultures shape characters, then it is too broad and imprecise. "We would do better," Meeks advises, "to adopt the cultural-linguistic model more self-consciously and, accordingly, to cast our descriptive net more broadly."[17] Nonetheless, it is possible to examine biblical narrative using the techniques of literary criticism. That is a use of narrative that is legitimate, precise, and useful.

Second, if narrative is going to be used as a term of cultural analysis, it may be necessary to focus on "sub-narratives" within the larger narrative. For example, were one to speak of the narrative of "America," would it not be necessary to consider the narratives of the various ethnic, religious, regional, political, and economic communities that make up American society? The sub-narrative may represent a distinctive reading of the larger narrative or even a kind of counter-narrative. Analogous developments are evident in Christian theology, where black, feminist, and liberation theologians argue that the experience or stories of their groups qualify their interpretation of the Christian tradition as a whole. If this process were carried further—say, to the point of distinguishing between the sub-narrative of descendants of slaves in the South and that of black immigrants from the Caribbean in New York City—narrative analysis might become unwieldy. Yet, it seems necessary if narrative analysis is to fulfill its intended purpose of taking diversity and particularity into account. My point is simply that the relation between narrative and sub-narrative deserves attention in any narrative program.

Third, we have seen Hauerwas fault political liberalism for its pretense that "we are free to the extent we have no story." The liberal narrative is said to be one that tells us that narratives are unimportant. This may not be true. Liberalism may indeed have narratives that display virtues like tolerance and respect for persons. Some of these narratives (e.g., novels such as Harriet Beecher Stowe's *Uncle Tom's Cabin*, George Eliot's *Daniel Deronda*, E. M. Forster's *Passage to India*, John Steinbeck's *Grapes of Wrath*, Alan Paton's *Cry, the Beloved Country,* as well as biographies and histories) have exerted considerable influence and shaped character.[18] Hauerwas, MacIntyre, and others may wish to reject liberal ideas, theories, and values, but they ought not assume *a priori* that they have not been and cannot be narrated. Indeed, the narratives of "liberal individualism" and "liberal democracy" might be a fertile field for further investigation.

Fourth, theologians wishing to employ narrative within the cultural-linguistic model of religion must rise to the challenge of their critics that they are weak on truth claims. They need to show, not only that their conception of theology allows for strong truth claims (as I think they have), but how truth claims might be defended. And, of course, they must do so without abandoning the tenets of postliberal theology. I believe this can be done and should be given a high priority on postliberalism's list of "things to do."

Fifth, postliberal theological ethicists need to ponder the ambiguities and problems identified in Hauerwas's work. Can vision, virtue, character, and narrative be brought into a stable coherence that exhibits our situated freedom? Narrative theological ethics needs to show more clearly how and on what basis we are able to choose among the various stories that claim our allegiance or compete for our attention. It needs to deal more forthrightly with the charge that it yields a vicious relativism. And, finally, it needs to demonstrate how an ethic of virtue and character shaped by narrative can be applied to very specific questions in social ethics.

Whether this program succeeds may depend upon the persuasiveness of a "two-tiered" account of morality encompassing both narratives and narrative-independent moral rules. To describe and defend such an account would be a daunting task and, if successful, a major achievement. However, as MacIntyre indicates, it would not be necessary to aspire to absolute justification but only to demonstrate that it is "the best theory so far" according to the criteria he sets forth.

Therefore, my sixth agenda item calls for further attention to ways in which the idea of society generates a core content for morality. Hobbes, Kant, Gert, Strawson, and the social sciences may be valuable sources. In any case, it would be necessary to limn the dimensions of the narrative-independent tier of morality and to show precisely how it connects with the narrative-dependent tier. Of course, the narrative story of the moral duplex is, as yet, only roughed in. So both require finishing. But the narrative-independent foundation cannot be so self-sufficient that the narrative aspect is only a decorative supplement. If narrative is to have a role beyond that which Braithwaite allows, then the relation between the two tiers will have to be one of genuine complementarity.

Much more than this cannot be said without actually doing it. For example, whether each tier would simply compensate for a deficiency in the other, or whether they would interpenetrate and qualify each other as love is sometimes said to reach down and "transform justice," remains an open question. To speak less abstractly about this two-tiered morality is an assignment for another day.

It may seem quixotic to contemplate staking out a common ground between foundationalism and antifoundationalism. Perhaps it is. But without some, at least minimal, common morality, "our sectarian, self-contained [narratives may] be reduced to communicating by driving large quantities of explosives into public places."[19]

NOTES

CHAPTER 1

1. Alasdair MacIntyre, "Moral Philosophy: What Next?" in *Revisions: Changing Perspectives in Moral Philosophy*, ed. Stanley Hauerwas and Alasdair MacIntyre, 4.
2. Gustafson, *Protestant and Roman Catholic Ethics*, 61ff.

CHAPTER 2

1. MacIntyre, *After Virtue*, 205, 208, 215.
2. Ibid., 216.
3. Gallie, *Philosophy and Historical Understanding*, 66.
4. Ibid., 70.
5. Ibid., 71, 66.
6. Mink, "The Divergence of History and Sociology in Recent Philosophy of History," 735. For the following account of these issues, I am indebted to this fine essay.
7. Ibid.
8. Fain, *Between Philosophy and History*, 261–62.
9. Arthur Danto and Morton White, who also have explored the place of narrative form in history, do not follow Gallie in rejecting entirely the covering-law model of explanation. See Danto, *Analytic Philosophy of History*, and Morton White, *Foundations of Historical Knowledge*.
10. Walzer, *Exodus and Revolution*, x, 7.

11. MacIntyre, *After Virtue*, 216.

12. MacIntyre, *A Short History of Ethics*, 269.

13. Anscombe, "Modern Moral Philosophy," 175.

14. MacIntyre, *After Virtue*, 11 and 12.

15. Ibid., 33.

16. Ibid., 34, 35.

17. Ibid., 13.

18. Ibid., 14.

19. Ibid., 16.

20. Ibid., 16, 17, 18.

21. See Santurri, "The Flight to Pragmatism," 336.

22. MacIntyre, *After Virtue*, 269.

23. MacIntyre's views regarding universalizability and prescriptivity appear in an early essay entitled "What Morality Is Not." See MacIntyre, *Against the Self-Images of the Age*. Universalizability cannot be a logically necessary feature of morality, simply because there are many cases in which persons making moral valuations "consciously refrain from legislating for others, although they might have done so; where a man says, for example, 'I ought to abstain from participation in war, but I cannot criticize or condemn responsible nonpacifists,' but might have said, 'One ought to abstain from participation in war' " (99). Such restraint can itself be motivated by moral considerations, and not merely reflect a speaker's apathy or timidity. It is also possible, as Iris Murdoch suggests, that someone may consider his or her duty to be unique—as something that pertains only to themselves because of who they are. MacIntyre's third objection is that universalizability renders certain acts of moral heroism unintelligible. One could never say that one ought to perform some act of supererogation if universalizability were required, because, in that case, one would be doing no more than one's duty—what anyone ought to do in similar circumstances. In any case, universalizability seems plausible only if one confines one's attention to that area of morality that consists of rules. MacIntyre, following Isaiah Berlin, observes that universalizability generally adheres to rules, whether moral or non-moral, and not to morality as such. The realm of the moral includes other things besides establishing rules and giving advice. When these other functions of morality (expressions of emotions, exhortation, persuasion, appraisal, and expression of one's own principles) are remembered, in MacIntyre's estimation, the attraction of universalizable prescription as an analysis of the essence of morality diminishes. Of course, I do not mean to suggest that MacIntyre has defeated prescriptivism or that its signal proponents (e.g., R. M. Hare) do not have cogent replies to his objections. An attempt to adjudicate this dispute is beyond the scope of this book, although some of the issues will be addressed in the next chapter.

24. MacIntyre, *After Virtue*, 21.

25. Gewirth, *Reason and Morality*, 171.

26. This objection is raised by R. M. Green in "Reason and Morality." The "conceptual relation" between needs/goods and rights is questioned by Millard Schumaker in "The Pain of Self-Contradiction."

27. MacIntyre, *After Virtue*, 67.

28. Ibid., 8, 10.

29. Of course, as Gene Outka has suggested to me, even if such "conceptual dependence" were to be acknowledged, it is not clear that the arguments would be any less "impersonal." After all, Kant and Aquinas themselves offered "impersonal" arguments.

30. MacIntyre, *After Virtue,* 10.

31. Ibid., 253.

32. Ibid. MacIntyre cites the Supreme Court's decision in the Bakke case as an example of this truce-keeping function.

33. Whether the fabric of moral discourse in the United States was ever intact and to what extent MacIntyre may idealize the past and exaggerate the perils of modernity are interesting questions that cannot be addressed here.

CHAPTER 3

1. Phillips and Mounce, *Moral Practices,* 14.

2. Ibid.

3. Ibid., 8.

4. Beardsmore, *Moral Reasoning,* 44.

5. See Winch, *Ethics and Action,* 50–72.

6. Phillips and Mounce, *Moral Practices,* 58–59.

7. Braithwaite, "An Empiricist's View of the Nature of Religious Belief," 78.

8. Ibid., 79.

9. Ibid., 80.

10. Ibid., 84.

11. Ibid., 85.

12. Ibid., 86.

13. Ibid. As R. W. Hepburn observes, Braithwaite's analysis is weak if it purports to describe the self-understanding of traditional historical Christianity. See Hepburn, "Vision and Choice in Morality," 194.

14. Braithwaite, "An Empiricist's View of the Nature of Religious Belief," 86.

15. Ibid., 89.

16. Ibid., 90.

17. Hepburn, "Vision and Choice in Morality," 181.

18. Ibid., 182.

19. Ibid., 184.

20. Ibid., 187.

21. Ibid.

22. Ibid., 189.

23. Ibid., 191.

24. Ibid., 192.

25. Ibid., 193.

26. Murdoch, "Vision and Choice in Morality," 199.

27. Ibid., 202.

28. Ibid., 203.

29. Ibid., 212, 214.

30. Ibid., 206, 208.

31. Ibid., 217. Whether this recommendation is compatible with her Platonism is an interesting question.

32. Ibid., 205. I do not wish to suggest, here or elsewhere, that there are not significant differences between Murdoch and MacIntyre. Murdoch remains, perhaps, more of a Platonist than a historicist.

33. Ibid., 204–5, 215.

34. For a more complete discussion (and one to which I shall return in the next chapter), see Frei, The Eclipse of Biblical Narrative, 13–14, and Kelsey, The Uses of Scripture in Recent Theology, 46–47.

35. Outka, "Character, Vision and Narrative," 115.

36. Berger, Invitation to Sociology, 176.

37. For confirmatory analyses of freedom, see Frankfurt, "Freedom of the Will and the Concept of a Person," 7, and Taylor, "Responsibility for Self," 287.

38. Beardsmore, Moral Reasoning, 54, 55.

39. MacIntyre's account of rebellion, discussed in the next chapter, may allow less freedom.

40. Donagan, The Theory of Morality, 9.

41. Ibid., 16, 17.

42. Gert, The Moral Rules, 80.

43. Ibid., 96.

44. Ibid., 133.

45. When Gert and, to anticipate, Strawson speak of moral ideals, they seem to refer primarily, if not exclusively, to individuals' ideals. Of course, Gert does mention religious ideals, and Strawson will refer to the ideals of moral communities, both of which are social. Nevertheless, I want to acknowledge that my references to social ideals and ideals presented by communal narratives may go beyond anything Gert or Strawson explicitly envision.

46. Strawson, "Social Morality and Individual Ideal," 283.

47. Ibid., 284. For a sensitive appraisal of Strawson's account that questions the adequacy of his "spheres," see Mitchell, Morality: Religious and Secular, 47–63.

48. Strawson, "Social Morality and Individual Ideal," 284, 291, 292.

49. Ibid., 294, 295.

50. Murdoch, "Vision and Choice in Morality," 209, 211.

51. For this interpretive point, I am indebted to Jeffrey Stout.

52. Gallie, "Liberal Morality and Socialist Morality," 133.

53. Phillips and Mounce, Moral Practices, 70–71.

54. Ibid., 73.

55. Ibid., 105.

56. Ibid., 107.

57. Ibid., 108.

58. Ibid.

59. Ibid., 111.

60. Hepburn, "Vision and Choice in Morality," 190.

61. MacIntyre, "Can Medicine Dispense with a Theological Perspective on Human Nature?," 40.

CHAPTER 4

1. The adjectives are those of Williams, *Ethics and the Limits of Philosophy,* 9.
2. MacIntyre, *After Virtue,* 121, 124, 125, 174.
3. Ibid., 186.
4. Ibid., 187.
5. Ibid., 188.
6. Ibid., 190.
7. Ibid., 191, 193.
8. Ibid., 194.
9. Ibid., 196.
10. Ibid., 187, 219.
11. Ibid., 219. Below I shall observe that MacIntyre's appeal to a human *telos* is rendered problematic by his emphasis on practices.
12. Ibid.
13. Ibid., 222.
14. Ibid.
15. Ibid., 216.
16. Ibid., 223.
17. Ibid., 263.
18. Williams, *Ethics,* 10.
19. Ibid., 11.
20. For these observations I am indebted to Stanley Hauerwas.
21. Williams, *Ethics,* 206.
22. MacIntyre, *After Virtue,* 223–24.
23. Ibid., 224. Stanley Hauerwas, as will be shown in Chapter 7, is equally reluctant to give up this possibility.
24. That some contemporary theologians make the same attempt with similar results will be demonstrated in the next chapter.
25. MacIntyre, *After Virtue,* 277.
26. Ibid., 221.
27. Ibid., 151.
28. Ibid.
29. Ibid., 276.
30. Ibid., 277.
31. See Williams, *Ethics,* 220.
32. Barber, "The World We Have Lost," 30–31.
33. Ibid., 31.
34. MacIntyre, *After Virtue,* 270.
35. Ibid.
36. Ibid., 271.
37. Williams, *Ethics,* 53.

CHAPTER 5

1. Goldberg, *Theology and Narrative,* 34.
2. Ibid., 35.

3. Stroup, *The Promise of Narrative Theology*, 71.
4. Niebuhr, *The Meaning of Revelation*, 36.
5. Ibid., 47, 52, 53.
6. Ibid., 34–35.
7. Lindbeck, *The Nature of Doctrine*, 16.
8. Ibid.
9. Ibid., 33.
10. Frei, "Theology and the Interpretation of Narrative," 1, 2.
11. Ibid., 2.
12. Ibid., 3.
13. Ibid., 3, 11.
14. Lindbeck, *The Nature of Doctrine*, 48.
15. Ibid., 50.
16. For an account of the last option, see Mitchell, *The Justification of Religious Belief*.
17. For discussion of these and related issues, see the articles by William C. Placher, Colman O'Neil, O.P., James J. Buckley, and David Tracy in *The Thomist* 49 (1985): 392–472; those of Charles M. Wood and Timothy P. Jackson in *Religious Studies Review* 11 (1985): 235–45; and that of Michael Root in *Dialog* 25 (1986): 175–80.
18. Crites, "The Narrative Quality of Experience," 301–2.
19. Ibid., 295, 296.
20. For the following survey of some of the literature, I am indebted to Goldberg's *Theology and Narrative* and to George Stroup for his *Promise of Narrative Theology* and "Bibliographical Critique."
21. Among these works, Sam Keen's *To a Dancing God*, Harvey Cox's *Seduction of the Spirit*, and Michael Novak's *Ascent of the Mountain, Flight of the Dove* are, perhaps, the most widely known. For references to these and others, see either of the works by Stroup cited in note 20.
22. Stroup, *The Promise of Narrative Theology*, 72. I quote at length because Stroup's description is, on the basis of my reading of this literature, accurate and illustrative of the endemic ambiguity.
23. Jenson, *Story and Promise*, 1.
24. Stroup, *The Promise of Narrative Theology*, 73.
25. Harned, *Creed and Personal Identity*, 8, 23, 76, 96.
26. Among these authors are Sam Keen, Harvey Cox, Richard Rubenstein, Michael Novak, Will Campbell, and William Sloane Coffin.
27. McClendon, *Biography as Theology*.
28. See Stroup, *The Promise of Narrative Theology*, 75–79; Goldberg, *Theology and Narrative*, 62–116; and Stanley Hauerwas with David B. Burrell, "Self-Deception and Autobiography: Reflections on Speer's *Inside the Third Reich*," in *Truthfulness and Tragedy: Further Investigations into Christian Ethics*, 82–98.
29. Estess, "The Inerrable Contraption," 433.
30. Stroup, "A Bibliographical Critique," 134.
31. Frei, *The Eclipse of Biblical Narrative*, 1.
32. Ibid., 2, 3.

33. Ibid., 6.

34. Ibid., viii. Frei cites Barth's figural interpretation of the Old Testament (*Church Dogmatics* II/2, pp. 340–409) and his narrative treatment of the gospel story (IV/1, pp. 224–28) as cases in point.

35. Kelsey, *The Uses of Scripture in Recent Theology*, 48–49.

36. Frei, "An Afterword: Eberhard Busch's Biography of Karl Barth," 114.

37. Lindbeck, "Theologische Methode und Wissenschaftstheorie" (p. 19 of English typescript).

38. Frei, *The Identity of Jesus Christ*, 94.

39. Ibid., 149.

40. Frei, "Theology and the Interpretation of Narrative," 27–28.

41. See Ricoeur, *Essays on Biblical Interpretation; Hermeneutics and the Human Sciences*; and the first two installments of his three-volume work *Time and Narrative*.

42. See Comstock, "Truth or Meaning."

43. Goldberg, *Theology and Narrative*, 12. Yet it is noteworthy that in his more recent constructive work he, himself, explores narratives' "ability to ring true" and shape lives without investigating their historical truth. He is content to assume their "general historicity." The stories' credibility can survive historical doubts about various details. See Goldberg, *Jews and Christians, Getting Our Stories Straight*, 220.

44. Goldberg, *Theology and Narrative*, 245.

45. Frei, *The Eclipse of Biblical Narrative*, 12.

46. Frei, *The Identity of Jesus Christ*, xiii.

47. Ibid., 51.

48. Stroup, *The Promise of Narrative Theology*, 88–89.

49. Ibid., 90, 91, 96, 239.

50. Ibid., 87, 205.

51. For example, Rorty, *Philosophy and the Mirror of Nature*; Stout, *The Flight from Authority*; and the recent work of Alasdair MacIntyre.

52. Stroup, *The Promise of Narrative Theology*, 175, 167.

53. Ibid., 153.

54. Ibid., 228–29.

55. Ibid., 231–32.

56. William C. Placher argues that postliberal theology is actually more "public" than liberal or "revisionist" theology in that "it understands a religion as fundamentally a public, communal activity, not a matter of the individual's experience" and no less "public" in terms of its capacity to "effectively address political and social issues." See his "Revisionist and Postliberal Theologies and the Public Character of Theology," 407.

57. See Stout, "The Voice of Theology in Contemporary Culture."

58. As an undergraduate "cultured despiser" once expressed, in the idiom of a then current cigarette ad, his surprising (even to himself) greater admiration for Barth than for Tillich: "Why smoke 'em if you can't taste 'em?" For a recent discussion of apologetics sensitive to the issues raised in this chapter, see Werpehowski, "Ad Hoc Apologetics."

59. Thiemann, *Revelation and Theology*, 91.

CHAPTER 6

1. Stroup, *The Promise of Narrative Theology,* 27.
2. Jack T. Sanders, *Ethics in the New Testament,* 130.
3. Birch and Rasmussen, *Bible and Ethics in the Christian Life,* 45–46.
4. *Interpreter's Dictionary of the Bible,* s.v. "Biblical Theology, Contemporary."
5. Kelsey, *The Uses of Scripture in Recent Theology,* 202–3, provides a conceptual typology of some traditional options.
6. Stendahl, "The Apostle Paul and the Introspective Conscience of the West," is a good example. Another is Richard A. Horsley's demonstration that Jesus' saying "love your enemies" does not pertain to non-violence or call for Christian pacifism. See his "Ethics and Exegesis."
7. *Interpreter's Dictionary of the Bible,* s.v. "Biblical Theology, Contemporary."
8. Kelsey, *Uses of Scripture,* 199.
9. Houlden, *Ethics and the New Testament,* vii–24.
10. In a similar listing, John H. Yoder, *The Politics of Jesus,* 16–17, also notes that Jesus was "a simple rural figure" and that he and his early followers "could not conceive of the exercise of social responsibility in any form other than that of simply being a faithful witnessing community."
11. Meeks, "Understanding Early Christian Ethics," 7.
12. Houlden, *Ethics,* 124, 24, 116.
13. Ibid., 120.
14. Ibid., 122.
15. Furnish, *The Love Command in the New Testament,* 214–15, 216.
16. Furnish, *The Moral Teaching of Paul,* 28.
17. Childs, *Biblical Theology in Crisis,* 131, 132.
18. Ibid., 134, 137.
19. Gustafson, *Theology and Christian Ethics,* 121–45. While Gustafson's account overlaps an earlier effort by Edward L. Long ["The Use of the Bible in Christian Ethics"], it is more detailed, subtle, and comprehensive. Since then, several more noteworthy studies have appeared: Verhey, "The Uses of Scripture in Ethics" and his *Great Reversal: Ethics and the New Testament;* and Spohn, *What Are They Saying About Scripture and Ethics?* See also Everding and Wilbanks, *Decision Making and the Bible,* and Birch and Rasmussen, *Bible and Ethics in the Christian Life.*
20. Kelsey, "Appeals to Scripture in Theology."
21. Gustafson, *Theology and Christian Ethics,* 129.
22. Ibid., 133.
23. Ibid., 134.
24. Curran, *Catholic Moral Theology in Dialogue.*
25. Ibid., 56, 64 and 54.
26. Gustafson, *Theology and Christian Ethics,* 148, 151.
27. Ogletree, *The Use of the Bible in Christian Ethics,* 7, 118.
28. Ibid., 3.
29. Hauerwas, *A Community of Character,* 68, 65.
30. Ibid., 66, 67.
31. Ibid., 69. Ironically, as Horsley shows, it may be Hauerwas who finds in the Bible what he wants to hear, at least in regard to love of enemies. See n. 6.

32. Ibid., 71.
33. Childress, "Scripture and Christian Ethics," 371, 372–73.
34. Ibid., 377, 376.
35. Ibid., 378, 379.
36. Ibid., 380.
37. Scholes and Kellogg, *The Nature of Narrative*, 4.
38. Kermode, *The Sense of an Ending*, 7.
39. Ibid., 6.
40. Kort, *Narrative Elements and Religious Meaning*, 19, 1, 17.
41. Ibid., 39, 79, 56, and 104.
42. Ibid., 111.
43. Auerbach, *Mimesis*, 23.
44. Ibid., 43.
45. Ibid., 15.
46. Ibid., 14–15. For other illuminating literary analyses of the Bible, see Alter, *The Art of Biblical Narrative*, and Frye, *The Great Code*.
47. James A. Sanders, *Torah and Canon*, 4.
48. Wilder, *Early Christian Rhetoric*, 56.
49. Stroup, "A Bibliographical Critique," 138. I am indebted to this helpful survey of the literature.
50. Funk, *Language, Hermeneutic, and the Word of God*, 158, cited by Stroup, p. 138. Stroup also numbers Gerhard Ebeling, Emil Fuchs, Dan O. Via, and Sallie McFague among the proponents of this view.
51. Stroup, "A Bibliographical Critique," 138.
52. William A. Beardslee, Norman Perrin, and Theodore Weeden are cited by Stroup.
53. Among the recent books are David Rhoads and Donald Michie, *Mark as Story: An Introduction to the Narrative of a Gospel* (Philadelphia: Fortress Press, 1982); Dan O. Via, Jr., *The Ethics of Mark's Gospel: In the Middle of Time* (Philadelphia: Fortress Press, 1985); Ernest Best, *Mark: The Gospel as Story* (Edinburgh: T. & T. Clark, 1985); and Jack Dean Kingsbury, *Matthew as Story* (Philadelphia: Fortress Press, 1985).
54. Via, *Ethics of Mark's Gospel*, 7.
55. Ibid., 174.
56. Barth, *Church Dogmatics* II/2, p. 706.
57. Kermode, *The Genesis of Secrecy*, 3.
58. Kermode, "Secrets and Narrative Sequence," 86. Kermode's article and those that accompany it were read at a symposium, "Narrative: The Illusion of Sequence," and have been republished in *On Narrative*, ed. W. J. T. Mitchell (Chicago: University of Chicago Press, 1981).
59. Walzer, *Exodus and Revolution*, 8.

CHAPTER 7

1. They are the co-editors of a series of books on ethics, including *Revisions: Changing Perspectives in Moral Philosophy*.

2. Hauerwas, *Character and the Christian Life*, 3–4. For a compelling counter-argument that Barth's ethics does allow for character see Werpehowski, "Command and History in the Ethics of Karl Barth."

3. Hauerwas, *Character*, 11.

4. Hauerwas, *The Peaceable Kingdom*, 17. But note that "Christian ethics as such is not in principle methodologically different from other ethics" (69).

5. Hauerwas, *Vision and Virtue*, 71.

6. Hauerwas, *Character*, vii. This is noted by Thomas W. Ogletree, "Character and Narrative," 25. However, Ogletree believes that in fact "the conceptual center of his thought is not character or virtue as such, but rather the notion of vision, and more particularly narrative and story; character and virtue are . . . correlated with these more basic notions" (28).

7. The tensions between these themes are identified and explored in Outka, "Character, Vision and Narrative."

8. Wary that "narrative theology" threatens to become a fad, Hauerwas claims that "it is a mistake to assume that my emphasis on narrative is the central focus of my position" (Hauerwas, *Peaceable Kingdom*, xxv). Yet he confesses he wants to be one of those theologians George Lindbeck says "desire to renew in a posttraditional and postliberal mode the ancient practice of absorbing the universe into the biblical world" through "typological, figurative, and narrative theology" (Hauerwas, *Against the Nations*, 1).

9. Hauerwas with Bondi and Burrell, *Truthfulness and Tragedy*, 74, 78, 76.

10. Ibid., 28–29.

11. Hauerwas, *Peaceable Kingdom*, xxi.

12. Hauerwas, *Against the Nations*, 2.

13. That some adjustments are needed will be evident below when I discuss the recurring philosophical issues.

14. Hauerwas, *A Community of Character*, 64.

15. Hauerwas lists a number of moral themes or virtues displayed in the narratives. Among them are hope, patience, courage, faithfulness, forgiveness, truthfulness, hospitality, leadership, and being adventuresome.

16. Hauerwas, *A Community of Character*, 57 and 59. It is difficult to see how this is consistent with his earlier observation that "stories without principles will have no way of concretely specifying the actions and practices consistent with the general orientation expressed by the story" (Hauerwas, *Vision and Virtue*, 89).

17. Hauerwas, *A Community of Character*, 241. Reinhold Niebuhr's ethic of "self-sacrificial love" might be, for Hauerwas, an equally "classic" example. Whether Ramsey's use of scripture has been uniform throughout his long career is a matter I cannot pursue here. However, it seems to me that in his earlier writings Ramsey's approach was similar to that advocated by Childress. Yet, in his recent work, Ramsey advances views that are somewhat different. In sum, it is unclear to what extent Childress and Ramsey really differ. See also Hauerwas, *Suffering Presence*, 72.

18. Hauerwas, *A Community of Character*, 58.

19. Ramsey, "A Question (or Two) for Stanley Hauerwas," 7, 9.

20. Ibid., 8.

21. See Hauerwas, *Peaceable Kingdom*, 4.

22. Kelsey, *The Uses of Scripture in Recent Theology*, 199.

23. Ogletree, "Character and Narrative," 26. The weaknesses of perfectionist theories are identified in Ogletree, *The Use of the Bible in Christian Ethics*, 33.

24. The quotations in this paragraph are from Hauerwas, *Peaceable Kingdom*, 93–95.

25. Outka, "Character, Vision and Narrative," 111. "What lies 'at the center of the idea of character' is the fact that each person has the capacity to be an agent; and to believe that character is important is 'to be normatively committed to the idea that it is better ... to shape than to be shaped'." The enclosed quotations are from Hauerwas, *Character*, 17–18.

26. Hauerwas, *Character*, 102; cited in Outka, "Character," 111. See also Hauerwas, *Peaceable Kingdom*, 96–97.

27. Outka, "Character," 112.

28. Hauerwas, Letter to Gene Outka, 17 March 1980. For a similar statement, see A *Community of Character*, 257, and *Peaceable Kingdom*, 39–43.

29. Ogletree, "Character and Narrative," 26.

30. Hauerwas, *Vision and Virtue*, 37 and 44.

31. Outka, "Character," 114. But see Hauerwas, *Peaceable Kingdom*, 43.

32. Outka, "Character," 115.

33. Kelsey, *Uses of Scripture*, 39–47.

34. Hauerwas, *Truthfulness and Tragedy*, 19.

35. Ibid., 35.

36. Ibid., 33.

37. Outka, "Character," 116.

38. Goldberg, *Theology and Narrative*, 143.

39. Robbins, "On the Role of Vision in Morality," 628, 629.

40. Hauerwas, *Vision and Virtue*, 74.

41. Robbins, "On the Role of Vision," 631.

42. Ibid., 633.

43. Hauerwas, "Learning to See Red Wheelbarrows," 649.

44. Robbins, "On the Role of Vision," 635.

45. Hauerwas, "Learning to See," 650.

46. Ibid.

47. Hauerwas, *Truthfulness and Tragedy*, 22, 23, 24–25.

48. Hauerwas, *Vision and Virtue*, 72.

49. Hauerwas, "Learning to See," 648.

50. Quoted in Hauerwas, *Vision and Virtue*, 83.

51. Hauerwas, "Learning to See," 649.

52. Ibid.

53. Hauerwas, *Truthfulness and Tragedy*, 58, 65.

54. Hauerwas, *Vision and Virtue*, 87, 85.

55. Hauerwas, *Truthfulness and Tragedy*, 35.

56. Hauerwas's essay on Albert Speer, "Self-Deception and Autobiography" (Ibid., 82–98), does little to alter this judgment. Had the Nazis not been defeated, would Speer have recognized his self-deception? Or what if, in defeat, he had reassured himself in the conviction that meaning transcends power? If our identi-

ties are as closely tied to our stories as Hauerwas maintains, it should be no surprise that we are inclined to be self-protective and uncritical of our narratives.

57. Hauerwas, *Truthfulness and Tragedy*, 9, 24, 35.

58. This summary is an extrapolation from a letter (22 May 1981) Hauerwas wrote to me in response to an earlier version of some of my questions and criticisms.

59. Hauerwas, *Truthfulness and Tragedy*, 72. See also the exchange between Julian Hartt, Hauerwas, and Crites in the *Journal of the American Academy of Religion* 52 (1984): 117–54, and Hauerwas, *Peaceable Kingdom*, 69.

60. Hauerwas, *Truthfulness and Tragedy*, 79, 38.

61. He maintains that he is an antifoundationalist and a historicist, but not a fideist or a relativist. See Hauerwas, *Against the Nations*, 4, 5, and 8.

62. Hauerwas, *A Community of Character*, 6. He does think there are Christians who embody the ethics he calls for.

63. Ibid., 1, 10.

64. Ibid., 73 and 3.

65. Hauerwas, *Peaceable Kingdom*, 106.

66. Hauerwas, *A Community of Character*, 2.

67. Ibid., 4. Also see Hauerwas, *Against the Nations*, 122–31.

68. Hauerwas, *A Community of Character*, 74, 84, 110.

69. Ibid., 85.

70. Ibid., 108.

71. Ibid., 83.

72. Ibid., 78.

73. Ibid., 78–82.

74. For some appreciative, yet guarded, comments about liberalism, see Hauerwas, *Against the Nations*, 18 and 122–31.

75. Hauerwas, *A Community of Character*, 12, 86.

76. Ibid., 86.

77. Ibid., 6. See Hauerwas, *Vision and Virtue*, 197–221. Hauerwas says that it is Christians "committed to the liberal values of the Enlightenment," and not he, who deserve to be called 'sectarian'. See Hauerwas, *Against the Nations*, 7.

78. Hauerwas, *A Community of Character*, 85. See also *Peaceable Kingdom*, 169, and *Against the Nations*, 7, among many others.

79. Hauerwas, *A Community of Character*, 82 and 109.

80. Ogletree, "Character and Narrative," 30.

81. Ibid. For his own view of Christian responsibility, see Ogletree, *The Use of the Bible*, 187–92.

82. Hauerwas, *A Community of Character*, 11.

83. Ibid., 247.

84. Ibid.

85. Hauerwas, *Peaceable Kingdom*, 75–76.

86. Ibid., 105–6.

87. Hauerwas, *Against the Nations*, 1.

88. Hauerwas, *Peaceable Kingdom*, 169.

89. Obviously I have not addressed the case Hauerwas makes on behalf of pacifism. My present interest is primarily methodological, though the issue does bear on the question of whether Hauerwas's ethic has sectarian and "withdrawal" implications. For a critique of his claim to biblical warrants for his pacifism, see Horsley, "Ethics and Exegesis."

90. A welcome exception to this is his most recent book, in which he recognizes an overlap between the Christian concern for care of the weak, the importance of gratitude, and a practice of medicine based on the Hippocratic Oath. See Hauerwas, *Suffering Presence*, 8 and 23–83.

91. Hauerwas, *A Community of Character*, 93.

92. Hauerwas, *Truthfulness and Tragedy*, 26. For positive statements about "the necessity" of Christian casuistry, see Hauerwas, *Peaceable Kingdom*, 120–22 and 130–31.

93. Hauerwas, *A Community of Character*, 3.

94. Hauerwas, *Suffering Presence*, 7, 18, and 125–56.

CHAPTER 8

1. Quoted in Hauerwas, *A Community of Character*, 160. For his most recent critique of "children's rights," see Hauerwas, *Suffering Presence*, 125–33.

2. Hauerwas, *A Community of Character*, 172, 165, 174, 176.

3. Ibid., 185, 191.

4. Ibid., 191. Dan O. Via, Jr., argues that the Gospel of Mark does not support Hauerwas's claims concerning the "political" function of marriage and Christian commitment to exclusive relationships. See Via, *The Ethics of Mark's Gospel*, 151–52.

5. Hauerwas, *A Community of Character*, 193.

6. Ibid., 190, 191.

7. The accuracy of Hauerwas's account of the early church's views and its relation to particular biblical texts is not my concern. My intention merely is to show the way in which Hauerwas understands his view of procreation to reflect the contours of Christian narrative (as he interprets it).

8. Hauerwas, *A Community of Character*, 191.

9. Ibid., 227. Also see Hauerwas, *Suffering Presence*, 147–49.

10. Hauerwas, *A Community of Character*, 165, 226.

11. Ramsey, "A Question (or Two) for Stanley Hauerwas," 18.

12. Ibid., 19.

13. Barth, *Church Dogmatics* III/4, p. 189.

14. Ramsey, "A Question," 33, 32.

15. Quoted in Johnson, *A Society Ordained by God*, 125.

16. Hauerwas says that, while Christians "seek forms of cooperation with [non-Christians] of good will," they must warn their partners that there are limits (e.g., violence in pursuit of justice) beyond which Christians will not go. Thus, he says, "we may not always be the ideal ally" (Hauerwas, *The Peaceable Kingdom*, 133).

17. Meeks, "Understanding Early Christian Ethics," 6.

18. I owe this observation to a presentation by John D. Barbour at the annual meeting of The American Academy of Religion, Dallas, December 1982. See Barbour, *Tragedy as a Critique of Virtue.*

19. I have adapted an image from Lovin, "Morality Amid the Ruins," 249.

BIBLIOGRAPHY

Alter, Robert. *The Art of Biblical Narrative.* New York: Basic Books, 1981.

Anscombe, G. E. M. "Modern Moral Philosophy." In *The Is-Ought Question,* edited by W. D. Hudson. New York: St. Martin's, 1969.

Auerbach, Erich. *Mimesis: The Representation of Reality in Western Literature.* Translated by W. R. Trask. Princeton: Princeton University Press, 1953.

Barber, Benjamin R. "The World We Have Lost." *The New Republic* (November 13, 1982): 30–31.

Barbour, John D. *Tragedy as a Critique of Virtue: The Novel and Ethical Reflection.* Chico, Calif.: Scholars Press, 1984.

Barth, Karl. *Church Dogmatics,* II/2, III/4, and IV/1. Translated by G. W. Bromiley et al. Edinburgh: T. & T. Clark, 1957, 1961, and 1965.

Beardsmore, R. W. *Moral Reasoning.* New York: Schocken Books, 1969.

Berger, Peter L. *Invitation to Sociology.* Garden City, N.Y.: Doubleday, 1963.

Birch, Bruce C., and Larry L. Rasmussen. *Bible and Ethics in the Christian Life.* Minneapolis: Augsburg Publishing House, 1976.

Braithwaite, R. B. "An Empiricist's View of the Nature of Religious Belief." In *The Philosophy of Religion,* edited by Basil Mitchell. London: Oxford University Press, 1971.

Buckley, James J. "Doctrine in the Diaspora." *The Thomist* 49 (1985): 443–59.

Childress, James F. "Scripture and Christian Ethics: Some Reflections on the Role of Scripture in Moral Deliberation and Justification." *Interpretation* 34 (1980): 371–80.

Childs, Brevard. *Biblical Theology in Crisis.* Philadelphia: Westminster Press, 1970.

Comstock, Gary. "Truth or Meaning: Ricoeur versus Frei on Biblical Narrative." *Journal of Religion* 66 (1986): 117–40.

Cox, Harvey. *The Seduction of the Spirit.* New York: Simon and Schuster, 1973.

Crites, Stephen. "The Narrative Quality of Experience." *Journal of the American Academy of Religion* 39 (1971): 291–311.

——. "A Respectful Reply to the Assertorical Theologian." *Journal of the American Academy of Religion* 52 (1984): 131–39.

Curran, Charles. *Catholic Moral Theology in Dialogue.* Notre Dame: University of Notre Dame Press, 1976.

Danto, Arthur C. *Analytic Philosophy of History.* Cambridge: Cambridge University Press, 1965.

Donagan, Alan. *The Theory of Morality.* Chicago: University of Chicago Press, 1977.

Estess, Ted L. "The Inerrable Contraption: Reflection on the Metaphor of Story." *Journal of the American Academy of Religion* 42 (1974): 415–34.

Everding, H. Edward, and Dana M. Wilbanks. *Decision Making and the Bible.* Valley Forge, Pa.: Judson Press, 1976.

Fain, Haskel. *Between Philosophy and History: The Resurrection of Speculative Philosophy of History within the Analytic Tradition.* Princeton: Princeton University Press, 1970.

Frankfurt, Harry G. "Freedom of the Will and the Concept of a Person." *The Journal of Philosophy* 68 (1971): 5–20.

Frei, Hans W. "An Afterword: Eberhard Busch's Biography of Karl Barth." In *Karl Barth in Review: Posthumous Works Reviewed and Assessed,* edited by H. Martin Rumscheidt. Pittsburgh: The Pickwick Press, 1981.

——. *The Eclipse of Biblical Narrative.* New Haven: Yale University Press, 1974.

——. *The Identity of Jesus Christ: The Hermeneutical Bases of Dogmatic Theology.* Philadelphia: Fortress Press, 1975.

——. "Theology and the Interpretation of Narrative: Some Hermeneutical Considerations." Paper presented at the annual meeting of the American Academy of Religion, New York, N.Y., December 20, 1982.

Frye, Northrup. *The Great Code: The Bible and Literature.* New York: Harcourt Brace Jovanovich, 1982.

Funk, Robert W. *Language, Hermeneutic, and the Word of God.* New York: Harper and Row, 1966.

Furnish, Victor Paul. *The Love Command in the New Testament.* Nashville: Abingdon Press, 1972.

——. *The Moral Teaching of Paul.* Nashville: Abingdon Press, 1979.

Gallie, W. B. "Liberal Morality and Socialist Morality." In *Philosophy, Politics and Society,* edited by Peter Laslett. Oxford: Blackwell, 1967.

——. *Philosophy and Historical Understanding.* New York: Schocken Books, 1968.

Gert, Bernard. *The Moral Rules.* New York: Harper & Row, 1966.

Gewirth, Alan. *Reason and Morality.* Chicago: University of Chicago Press, 1978.

Goldberg, Michael. *Jews and Christians, Getting Our Stories Straight.* Nashville: Abingdon Press, 1985.

———. *Theology and Narrative: A Critical Introduction.* Nashville: Abingdon Press, 1982.

Green, R. M. "Reason and Morality." *Religious Studies Review* 5 (1974): 187–90.

Gustafson, James M. *Protestant and Roman Catholic Ethics: Prospects for Rapprochement.* Chicago: University of Chicago Press, 1978.

———. *Theology and Christian Ethics.* Philadelphia: Pilgrim Press, 1974.

Harned, David B. *Creed and Personal Identity.* Philadelphia: Fortress Press, 1981.

Hartt, Julian. "Theological Investments in Story: Some Comments on Recent Developments and Some Proposals" and "Reply to Crites and Hauerwas." *Journal of the American Academy of Religion* 52 (1984): 117–30 and 149–56.

Hauerwas, Stanley. *Against the Nations: War and Survival in a Liberal Society.* Minneapolis: Winston Press, 1985.

———. *Character and the Christian Life: A Study in Theological Ethics.* San Antonio: Trinity University Press, 1975.

———. *A Community of Character: Toward a Constructive Social Ethic.* Notre Dame: University of Notre Dame Press, 1981.

———. "Learning to See Red Wheelbarrows: On Vision and Relativism." *Journal of the American Academy of Religion* 45 (1977): 643–55.

———. *The Peaceable Kingdom: A Primer in Christian Ethics.* Notre Dame: University of Notre Dame Press, 1983.

———. *Suffering Presence: Theological Reflections on Medicine, the Mentally Handicapped and the Church.* Notre Dame: University of Notre Dame Press, 1986.

———. *Vision and Virtue: Essays in Christian Ethical Reflection.* Notre Dame: Fides Publishers, 1974.

———. "Why the Truth Demands Truthfulness: An Imperious Engagement with Hartt." *Journal of the American Academy of Religion* 52 (1984): 141–47.

Hauerwas, Stanley, and Alasdair MacIntyre, eds. *Revisions: Changing Perspectives in Moral Philosophy.* Notre Dame: University of Notre Dame Press, 1983.

Hauerwas, Stanley, with Richard Bondi and David B. Burrell. *Truthfulness and Tragedy: Further Investigations into Christian Ethics.* Notre Dame: University of Notre Dame Press, 1977.

Hepburn, R. W. "Vision and Choice in Morality." In *Christian Ethics and Contemporary Philosophy,* edited by I. T. Ramsey. New York: Macmillan, 1966.

Horsley, Richard. "Ethics and Exegesis: 'Love your Enemies' and the Doctrine of Non-Violence." *Journal of the American Academy of Religion* 54 (1986): 3–31.

Houlden, J. L. *Ethics and the New Testament.* New York: Oxford University Press, 1977.

Jackson, Timothy P. "Against Grammar." *Religious Studies Review* 11 (1985): 241–45.

Jenson, Robert W. *Story and Promise.* Philadelphia: Fortress Press, 1973.

Johnson, James Turner. *A Society Ordained by God: English Puritan Marriage Doctrine in the First Half of the Seventeenth Century.* Nashville: Abingdon Press, 1970.

Keen, Sam. *To a Dancing God.* New York: Harper & Row, 1970.

Kelsey, David H. "Appeals to Scripture in Recent Theology." *Journal of Religion* 48 (1968): 1–21.

——. *The Uses of Scripture in Recent Theology.* Philadelphia: Fortress Press, 1975.

Kermode, Frank. *The Genesis of Secrecy: On the Interpretation of Narrative.* Cambridge: Harvard University Press, 1979.

——. "Secrets and Narrative Sequence." *Critical Inquiry* 7 (1980): 83–101.

——. *The Sense of an Ending: Studies in the Theory of Fiction.* New York: Oxford University Press, 1967.

Kort, Wesley A. *Narrative Elements and Religious Meaning.* Philadelphia: Fortress Press, 1975.

Lindbeck, George A. *The Nature of Doctrine: Religion and Theology in a Post-Liberal Age.* Philadelphia: Westminster Press, 1984.

——. "Theologische Methode und Wissenschaftstheorie." *Theologische Revue* 74 (1978): 266–79.

Long, Edward L. "The Use of the Bible in Christian Ethics." *Interpretation* 19 (1965): 149–62.

Lovin, Robin W. "Morality Amid the Ruins: Jeffrey Stout on the Failure of Authority and Autonomy." *Journal of Religion* 65 (1985): 244–49.

McClendon, James W. *Biography as Theology.* Nashville: Abingdon Press, 1974.

MacIntyre, Alasdair. *After Virtue: A Study in Moral Theory.* 2d ed. Notre Dame: University of Notre Dame Press, 1984.

——. *Against the Self-Images of the Age.* Notre Dame: University of Notre Dame Press, 1978.

——. "Can Medicine Dispense with a Theological Perspective on Human Nature?" In *Knowledge, Value and Belief,* edited by Tristram Engelhardt, Jr., and Daniel Callahan. Hastings-on-Hudson, N.Y.: The Institute of Society, Ethics and the Life Sciences, 1977.

——. *A Short History of Ethics.* New York: Macmillan, 1966.

Meeks, Wayne A. "Understanding Early Christian Ethics." *Journal of Biblical Literature* 105 (1986): 3–11.

Meilaender, Gilbert C. *The Theory and Practice of Virtue.* Notre Dame: University of Notre Dame Press, 1984.

Mink, L. O. "The Divergence of History and Sociology in Recent Philosophy of History." In *Logic, Methodology and Philosophy of Science,* Vol. 4. Edited by Patrick Suppes. Amsterdam: North-Holland Publishing Company, 1973.

Mitchell, Basil. *The Justification of Religious Belief.* New York: Seabury Press, 1973.

——. *Morality: Religious and Secular.* Oxford: Oxford University Press, 1980.

Mouw, Richard J. "Alasdair MacIntyre on Reformation Ethics." *The Journal of Religious Ethics* 13 (1985): 243–57.

Murdoch, Iris. "Vision and Choice in Morality." In *Christian Ethics and Contemporary Philosophy,* edited by I. T. Ramsey. New York: Macmillan, 1966.

Niebuhr, H. Richard. *The Meaning of Revelation.* New York: Macmillan, 1941.

Novak, Michael. *Ascent of the Mountain, Flight of the Dove.* New York: Harper & Row, 1971.

Ogletree, Thomas W. "Character and Narrative: Stanley Hauerwas' Studies of the Christian Life." *Religious Studies Review* 6 (1980): 25–30.

——. *The Use of the Bible in Christian Ethics.* Philadelphia: Fortress Press, 1983.

O'Niel, Colman, O.P. "The Rule Theory of Doctrine and Propositional Truth." *The Thomist* 49 (1985): 417–42.

Outka, Gene. "Character, Vision and Narrative." *Religious Studies Review* 6 (1980): 110–18.

Phillips, D. Z. *Through a Darkening Glass: Philosophy, Literature and Cultural Change.* Notre Dame: University of Notre Dame Press, 1982.

Phillips, D. Z., and H. O. Mounce. *Moral Practices.* New York: Schocken Books, 1970.

Placher, William C. "Revisionist and Postliberal Theologies and the Public Character of Theology." *The Thomist* 49 (1985): 392–416.

Ramsey, Paul. "A Question (or Two) for Stanley Hauerwas." Paper presented at a symposium convened by The Center for Theological Inquiry, Princeton, N.J., November 19–21, 1982.

Ricoeur, Paul. *Essays on Biblical Interpretation.* Philadelphia: Fortress Press, 1980.

——. *Hermeneutics and the Human Sciences.* Edited and translated by John B. Thompson. Cambridge: Cambridge University Press, 1981.

——. *Time and Narrative.* Vol. 1 and 2. Translated by Kathleen McLaughlin and David Pellauer. Chicago: University of Chicago Press, 1984 and 1985.

Robbins, J. Wesley. "On the Role of Vision in Morality." *Journal of the American Academy of Religion* 45 (1977): 623–41.

Root, Michael. "Truth, Relativism and Postliberal Theology." *Dialog* 25 (1986): 175–80.

Rorty, Richard. *Philosophy and the Mirror of Nature.* Princeton: Princeton University Press, 1981.

Sanders, Jack T. *Ethics in the New Testament.* Philadelphia: Fortress Press, 1975.

Sanders, James A. *Torah and Canon.* Philadelphia: Fortress Press, 1972.

Santurri, Edmund N. "The Flight to Pragmatism." *Religious Studies Review* 9 (1982): 330–38.

Scholes, Robert, and Robert Kellogg. *The Nature of Narrative.* Oxford: Oxford University Press, 1966.

Schumaker, Millard. "The Pain of Self-Contradiction." *Journal of Religion* 59 (1979): 352–56.

Spohn, William C., S.J. *What Are They Saying About Scripture and Ethics?* New York: Paulist Press, 1984.

Stendahl, Krister. "The Apostle Paul and the Introspective Conscience of the West." *Harvard Theological Review* 56 (1963): 199–215.

———. "Biblical Theology, Contemporary." In *Interpreter's Dictionary of the Bible,* 1. Nashville: Abingdon Press, 1962.

Stout, Jeffrey. *The Flight from Authority.* Notre Dame: University of Notre Dame Press, 1981.

———. "The Voice of Theology in Contemporary Culture." In *Religion and America: Spirituality in a Secular Age,* edited by Mary Douglas and Steven M. Tipton. Boston: Beacon Press, 1983.

Strawson, P. F. "Social Morality and Individual Ideal." In *Christian Ethics and Contemporary Philosophy,* edited by I. T. Ramsey. New York: Macmillan, 1966.

Stroup, George W. "A Bibliographical Critique." *Theology Today* 32 (1975): 133–43.

———. *The Promise of Narrative Theology.* Atlanta: John Knox Press, 1981.

Taylor, Charles. "Responsibility for Self." In *The Identities of Persons,* edited by A. O. Rorty. Berkeley: University of California Press, 1976.

Thiemann, Ronald F. *Revelation and Theology: The Gospel as Narrated Promise.* Notre Dame: University of Notre Dame Press, 1985.

Tracy, David. "Lindbeck's New Program for Theology." *The Thomist* 49 (1985): 460–72.

Verhey, Allen. *The Great Reversal: Ethics and the New Testament.* Grand Rapids: William B. Eerdmans, 1984.

———. "The Uses of Scripture in Ethics." *Religious Studies Review* 4 (1978): 28–38.

Via, Dan O., Jr. *The Ethics of Mark's Gospel — In the Middle of Time.* Philadelphia: Fortress Press, 1985.

Walzer, Michael. *Exodus and Revolution.* New York: Basic Books, 1985.

Werpehowski, William. "Ad Hoc Apologetics." *Journal of Religion* 66 (1986): 282–301.

———. "Command and History in the Ethics of Karl Barth." *Journal of Religious Ethics* 9 (1981): 298–320.

White, Morton. *Foundations of Historical Knowledge.* New York: Harper & Row, 1965.

White, R. E. O. *Biblical Ethics.* Atlanta: John Knox Press, 1979.

Wilder, Amos. *Early Christian Rhetoric: The Language of the Gospel.* Cambridge: Harvard University Press, 1971.

Williams, Bernard. *Ethics and the Limits of Philosophy.* Cambridge: Harvard University Press, 1985.

Winch, Peter. *Ethics and Action.* London: Routledge and Kegan Paul, 1972.

Wood, Charles M. "The Nature of Doctrine: Religion and Theology in a Postliberal Age by George A. Lindbeck." *Religious Studies Review* 11 (1985): 235–40.
Yoder, John H. *The Politics of Jesus.* Grand Rapids: William B. Eerdmans, 1972.
———. *The Priestly Kingdom: Social Ethics as Gospel.* Notre Dame: University of Notre Dame Press, 1984.

INDEX